# Towards a Brave New Arms Industry?

Richard A. Bitzinger

**ADELPHI PAPER** 356

Oxford University Press, Great Clarendon Street, Oxford OX2 6DP
Oxford New York
Athens Auckland Bangkok Bombay Calcutta Cape Town
Dar es Salaam Delhi Florence Hong Kong Istanbul Karachi
Kuala Lumpur Madras Madrid Melbourne Mexico City
Nairobi Paris Singapore Taipei Tokyo Toronto
and associated companies in
Berlin Ibadan

Oxford is a trade mark of Oxford University Press

Published in the United States
by Oxford University Press Inc., New York

© The International Institute for Strategic Studies 2003

**First published** May 2003 by **Oxford University Press** for
**The International Institute for Strategic Studies**
Arundel House, 13–15 Arundel Street, Temple Place, London WC2R 3DX
**www.iiss.org**

**Director** John Chipman
**Editor** Tim Huxley
**Copy Editor** Glen Quatermain
**Production** Shirley Nicholls, Simon Nevitt

British Library Cataloguing in Publication Data
Data available

Library of Congress Cataloguing in Publication Data

**ISBN** 0-19-852835-3
**ISSN** 0567-932x

Cover top image © Gripen International 2003

# Contents

# Tables and figures

# Introduction

The past decade has not been kind to the global arms industry. The end of the Cold War has resulted in a new international dynamic – military, political and economic – that has forced a severe retrenchment in defence industries among the major arms-producing countries. Despite the persistence of regional conflicts around the world, many of them involving the major powers, tensions in other parts of the globe have abated considerably, and with them has gone much of the need for large defence budgets and sizeable armed forces. As much of the world has disarmed and demilitarised, so too the demands – and budgets – for new weapon systems have declined.[1] To put it bluntly, the end of the Cold War has left the world with considerably more capacity and capability to develop and produce arms than it either needs or can afford.

The impact on the global arms industry has been undeniable. Among the large advanced arms-producing countries – the US, the UK and France, for instance – hundreds of thousands of defence workers have been made redundant as military factories have cut back production, or even closed. The industry has undergone an unprecedented restructuring, both on a national and a global scale. The number of major defence firms has declined dramatically as companies have either merged or purchased the military assets of other corporations leaving the defence business. During the 1990s, these mergers and acquisitions also began to cross national boundaries, as the emerging defence giants sought new partners and subsidiaries. Another by-product of the drop in domestic demand for arms has been the growing importance of exports as a source of compensatory revenues. The effects of these developments are still being felt; governments are wrestling with their implications for national security, domestic economic growth and development, and international relations.

However much the larger arms-producing states have been pummelled by these developments, the long-term viability of these countries' defence industries is not in doubt. Firms may contract, merge or globalise, and governments may be compelled to internationalise their arms procurement, but the large arms-producing countries are unlikely to lose their across-the-board capabilities. The same cannot, however, be said for the smaller, 'second-tier' countries. For them, the issue is not simply one of dealing with reduced demand and excess capacity, but increasingly of survival. In other words, can these lesser arms-producing states endure in an increasingly competitive and globalised arms marketplace, and if so, how?

This paper addresses the current dilemmas and likely future facing these so-called second-tier arms-producing states. By examining the experiences and reactions of a cross-section of these producers, the paper examines several issues. How have post-Cold War military, economic and technological challenges specifically affected these countries? How are secondary arms producers reacting to these challenges? Which strategies have been successful and which have not, and what are the lessons for other second-tier and aspiring arms producers? Finally, given unfolding trends and developments worldwide, what might the structure and character of the global arms industry look like 10-15 years from now?

While it has long been accepted that the global arms industry is hierarchical,[2] there is no generally-agreed definition of what constitutes a second-tier arms-producing country.[3] For the purposes of this paper, the *first-tier* of arms-producing states comprises the US, the UK, France, Germany and Italy. These five countries possess the world's largest and most technologically advanced defence industries, and together they account for roughly 75% of global armaments production.[4] Moreover, they dominate – either singularly or collectively – the global defence research and development (R&D) process. *Third-tier* states are those possessing limited and generally low-technology arms-production capabilities, such as Egypt, Mexico and Nigeria.

The *second-tier* arms producers comprise a diverse group of countries falling between these two categories. It includes industrialised countries possessing small but often quite sophisticated defence industries, such as Australia, Canada, the Czech Republic, Norway, Japan and Sweden. It also contains a number of developing or newly industrialised countries with modest military-industrial complexes, such as Argentina, Brazil, Indonesia, Iran, Israel, Singapore, South Africa, South Korea, Taiwan and Turkey. Finally, the second tier includes China and India – states with large, broad-based defence industries, but which still lack the independent R&D and industrial capacities to develop and produce highly sophisticated conventional arms.[5]

Despite being a rather catholic group, second-tier countries share a number of growing challenges to their arms industries as the political-military arguments for home-grown defence industries weaken, and as the economic and technological barriers to domestic arms production rise. The main thrust of this paper is that second-tier arms producers are being forced to rethink radically and recast their defence industries. For many, this means cancelling more ambitious indigenous programmes, and drastically retrenching and reorienting their arms industries. In addition, it means accepting a more integrated but subordinate role in an increasingly globalised and interdependent defence industry. Structurally, such a system could resemble a huge 'hub-and-spoke' model: a few large first-tier firms at the core, serving as 'centres of excellence' for weapons design, development and systems integration, with global supply chains extending out to second-tier states on the periphery. As a consequence of this rationalisation/globalisation process, a radically different global arms industry could be emerging, with profound consequences for proliferation and arms control.

While participation in such a global division of labour may bring new economic and technological benefits to many second-tier producers, it will also demand that they abandon their original objectives of autarky, or self-sufficiency, in arms development and manufacturing. For some countries, this will be a difficult adjustment. On the other hand, should they choose not to rationalise and globalise their defence industries, these countries will face the much more difficult challenge – with no assurance of success – of securing additional resources, technologies and markets in order to sustain local production.

This paper is divided into three chapters. The first examines why second-tier countries seek to establish their own defence industries. It identifies these countries' expectations of autarky, perceived economic benefits and 'technonationalism', or status and prestige, as the strongest motivations impelling defence industrialisation. It then examines how these countries have typically gone about building indigenous arms-production capabilities, paying particular attention to the gradualist/evolutionist model – the so-called 'ladder of production' – and the critical role of the state in nurturing domestic arms industries.

This chapter also addresses the myths and fallacies of indigenous arms production. It argues that self-sufficiency has largely been a shibboleth, and that most second-tier producers have failed to eliminate or even substantially reduce their subordination to foreign suppliers; rather, they have simply replaced one form of dependency (finished weapon systems) with another (critical military technologies and subsystems). This is largely due to continued deficiencies and weaknesses in these countries' technology and production bases, which have impeded progress up the ladder of production and often resulted in indigenous armaments being much less capable than foreign-sourced weaponry. In addition, the economic benefits of indigenous arms production have rarely lived up to expectations. Given high research, development and start-up costs, and typically low production runs, domestically produced arms have tended to be more expensive than imports. Meanwhile, optimistic goals for indigenous production have led to an over-expansion of most of these countries' defence industrial bases, resulting in over-capacity.

As a result, the capabilities for independent arms production among most second-tier countries have largely levelled off at a 'mid-tech' level – that is, capable of indigenously producing less sophisticated military equipment, such as armoured vehicles, trainer aircraft or patrol boats, or of licence-producing foreign-designed weapon systems, such as fighter jets or submarines. Yet given the reduced resources now available, even this level of capability is increasingly unsustainable. Therefore, this paper next examines, in its second chapter, the readjustments several secondary suppliers have made, and assesses their significance and prospects for success. These readjustments include: rationalising defence industries through reductions in the workforce, plant closures and company mergers and acquisitions; halting certain kinds of defence work; pursuing defence conversion or commercial diversification; leveraging dual-use technologies; and globalising defence industries via increased exports or internationalised production.

These case studies examine a spectrum of second-tier arms producers, including the smaller industrialised countries (Sweden), the developing world (Brazil and South Africa) and newly industrialised economies (NIEs) such as South Korea and Taiwan. In so doing, this chapter addresses a cross-section of second-tier circumstances and responses, and highlights differences and similarities in approach.

Finally, this paper describes the possible future structure and character of the global arms industry, and how the smaller producing states may fit into this system. It also addresses the implications and challenges that a more globalised and hierarchical defence industry will pose for international security, proliferation and arms-control policies, as well as how such an emerging international model of production may itself contain innovative answers to these challenges.

# Chapter 1

## The Rise and Fall of Second-Tier Arms Producers

Countries have several reasons for developing and producing their own arms. Perhaps the strongest of these is the security-driven imperative for self-sufficiency, or autarky, in arms procurement.[1] In a basically anarchic international security system, nation-states are naturally impelled to seek an independent defence capability. These considerations were particularly strong during the Cold War, when several second-tier producers perceived themselves to be facing proximate threats. Sweden, for example, was a non-aligned and neutral country wedged between two mutually antagonistic military blocs. Apartheid-era South Africa perceived challenges to its rule from within and without, while Israel, South Korea and Taiwan continue to face proximate regional threats. In order to defend its territory satisfactorily, therefore, a nation-state requires a reliable source of armaments, and the most dependable source is generally a domestic one.

In addition, relying too heavily on arms imports makes a country vulnerable to having supplies cut off, or technology held back. Embargoes, sanctions and other types of supplier restraints – whether real or potential – have tended to reinforce the perception of many states that they must establish a secure, *indigenous* source of armaments. During the Cold War, many second-tier arms producers favoured self-sufficiency and hedged against arms-export bans. South Africa initiated indigenous production in direct response to UN-imposed arms embargoes in 1963 and 1977. As a result, by the late 1980s Pretoria could claim to be '95 percent self-reliant' in military procurement, including fighter aircraft, armoured vehicles and artillery, and surface combatants.[2]

Israel's growing frustration with foreign arms suppliers during the 1960s and 1970s – including France's ban on sales in 1967 and Britain's cut-off in 1969 – only increased Tel Aviv's interest in securing a reliable, domestic source of armaments. This, in turn, prompted a heavy build-up of the indigenous defence industry. By the late 1980s, Israel was capable of building its own fighter jets, tanks and air-to-air and anti-ship cruise missiles, and it was a world leader in unmanned aerial vehicles (UAVs).[3]

Taiwan's growing diplomatic isolation from the late 1970s, and its subsequent fears about being cut off from its principal overseas arms suppliers, was a prime motivation for establishing an indigenous arms-producing capability. In the early 1980s, after the US refused to sell it the F-20 *Tigershark* aircraft, Taiwan began developing its Indigenous Defensive Fighter (IDF). In addition, US unwillingness to export the Advanced Medium-Range Air-to-Air Missile (AMRAAM) and the *Harpoon* anti-ship cruise missile prompted Taipei to develop its own such systems.

South Korea initiated its defence-industrialisation programme in 1974, after the promulgation of the Nixon Doctrine, which both reduced US defence commitments to Asia and liberalised the export of advanced military technologies to allies such as South Korea. As a result, by 1995 nearly 80% of South Korea's arms were procured domestically, including aircraft, armoured vehicles, warships and submarines.[4]

Sweden established its arms industry in accordance with its longstanding policy of neutrality and non-alignment. An independent defence-industrial capability was seen as central to preserving a credible military deterrent, as well as reducing its exposure to outside suppliers and the possible cut-off of vital arms during a crisis or conflict (as happened during the Second World War).[5] Consequently, by the late 1980s Sweden procured approximately 70% of its arms indigenously, including submarines, tanks, armoured vehicles, artillery, surface-to-air and anti-ship missiles and combat aircraft.[6]

China's unhappy experiences with foreign military-technical assistance – the abrupt cut-off of Soviet military aid in the early 1960s and the Western arms embargo following the 1989 Tiananmen Square massacre – reinforced Beijing's natural impulse to become self-reliant in arms production.[7] By the early 1970s, therefore, the

Chinese were developing indigenously designed weapon systems, and the country is now able to produce its own fighter aircraft, ballistic and anti-ship cruise missiles, tanks and submarines, among other weapon systems.

At the same time, a reduced reliance on foreign sources of arms was viewed as a means of strengthening national political independence. Dependencies on foreign supplies leave a buyer open to attempts by the supplier to withhold deliveries in order to coerce the purchaser into making concessions on national issues (such as human rights) or international issues (such as combating terrorism and drug trafficking or opposing a common regional threat). In Japan, for example, proponents of *kokusanka* (autonomy in arms production) perceived this industrial strategy as providing Tokyo with greater freedom of action in international affairs. At the same time, *kokusanka* arguably helped to strengthen Tokyo's security relationship with the US, permitting Japan to play a larger role in the bilateral alliance.[8]

In addition to fulfilling perceived requirements for self-sufficiency, arms production has often been seen as an important mechanism for driving a country's overall economic development and industrialisation. Defence industrialisation has potential backward linkages spurring the expansion and modernisation of other sectors of the national economy, such as steel, machine tools and shipbuilding.[9] Industrialisation and technological advancement were seen as feeding into the development of domestic arms-manufacturing capabilities, building up general skills and know-how, and in providing lead-in support or equipment for arms production. The construction of warships, for example, stimulated the establishment of indigenous ship-building industries, while the production of military vehicles required steel mills and automotive factories to provide critical parts and components, such as armour plating, chassis and engine manufacture, and skilled labour for vehicle assembly. Both Brazil and South Korea pursued parallel strategies of 'security and development', building up their heavy industry and high-technology sectors at the same time as they strove for self-sufficiency in arms production.[10]

As a result, in many second-tier states, armaments production has become a critical component in the national economy. China's vast military-industrial complex, for example, provides jobs for more than three million workers, engineers and technicians. These are engaged in over 1,000 enterprises, each constituting multiple factories, research institutes, trading companies, technical schools and universities, along with housing units, schools, day-care centres, hospitals and recreational centres.[11] At its peak in the late 1980s, South Africa's arms industry employed nearly 132,000 workers, accounting for 9% of the country's manufacturing employment and 1.5% of its gross national product (GNP). Armscor, South Africa's pre-eminent defence conglomerate, was one of the country's largest industrial groups.[12] During the 1980s, over 20% of Israel's industrial workforce was engaged in arms manufacturing, and for a time Israeli Aircraft Industries (IAI) was the country's largest single employer.[13] In Sweden, defence contracting employed one out of every ten workers in the machinery and metalworking industry, as well as 10% of the country's engineers.[14] Particularly during the Cold War, Sweden's long-ruling Social Democrats saw the local defence industry as a 'necessary evil', essential to maintaining full employment.[15]

At the same time, armaments production was viewed as a 'technology locomotive' spurring the growth of new industries and technologies, particularly in aerospace, electronics and information technology.[16] Military aerospace programmes, for example, constituted the basis for civil aircraft and aviation production in nearly all of the second-tier arms-producing states. For example, Brazil's Embraer (*Empresa Brasileira da Aeronautica*) – initially based on military-led industrialisation – subsequently expanded into the regional jet business. Sweden's Saab – originally a fighter-jet manufacturer – also branched out into the production of commuter planes in the 1980s, while Japan's aircraft companies have become major subcontractors to Boeing and Airbus commercial airliner programmes. Israel's high-technology sectors have also benefited greatly from cross-fertilisation with military industries,[17] and South Korea has attempted to exploit military-to-commercial spin-offs in its communications, electronics, machine-tool and transport sectors.[18]

Second-tier states saw domestic arms production as providing other economic benefits as well. Defence industrialisation could function as an import-substitution strategy; instead of sending capital (especially government monies) out of the country via arms imports, countries can use indigenous arms production to create jobs, ameliorate trade imbalances and protect foreign-currency reserves. Furthermore, by *exporting* arms, defence firms constituted an important source of foreign-currency earnings. Brazil in particular pursued an aggressive export-led defence-industrialisation strategy, and by the late 1980s had emerged as the world's largest exporter of wheeled armoured vehicles, as well as being a major supplier of lightweight trainer planes and multiple rocket launchers to a number of armed forces in Latin America, Africa, the Middle East and even Western Europe.[19] During the mid-1980s, Brazil was the sixth-largest arms exporter in the world.[20] The Swedish, Israeli, South African and Singaporean arms industries have also relied on overseas arms sales for a sizeable portion of their revenues. In fact, in the cases of South Africa and Israel, the local defence industry has been among the largest exporters of manufactured goods overall.[21]

Finally, nationalism, status and prestige also have an effect on defence industrialisation, particularly in the case of second-tier states that aspire to regional or even global great-power status.[22] Possessing an independent defence-industrial capability feeds directly into concepts of national power – not only by creating military power but also by demonstrating the country's industrial and technological prowess, thereby confirming its status as a great power in the broadest sense. Consequently, many aspiring great powers – such as Japan during the nineteenth century and the Soviet Union during the twentieth – have often devoted considerable resources to building up indigenous arms production. Today, would-be great powers such as China, India, Iran and Russia have also invested large quantities of time, money and manpower in domestic defence industrialisation.

This 'rich nation/strong army' complex is not confined to aspiring great powers, and such technonationalism can be detected in several smaller second-tier arms-producers, such as Argentina, Brazil, Indonesia, Israel and South Korea. Brazil's military leadership embarked on an ambitious defence-industrialisation programme in the 1960s based in part on the belief that a powerful army was unsustainable in the absence of a strong domestic arms industry.[23] Indonesia established an aviation industry as an indicator of its intentions to become a modern industrialised nation and a power to be reckoned with in Southeast Asia. South Korea pursued an advanced arms-production capability not only to repel an attack from North Korea, but also to position itself as a 'full-fledged player upon the regional stage', with a view that this would be of particular use after any future reunification.[24]

## The ladder of production and the role of the state in second-tier defence industrialisation

When countries – especially second-tier arms producers – decide to begin indigenously manufacturing arms, they have tended to follow similar patterns of industrialisation and production. This process usually entails a series of gradual and progressive steps leading to greater sophistication and self-sufficiency in the design, development and manufacture of weapon systems. As such, it has often been described as the 'ladder of production', and while scholars may disagree as to how many steps there are or the precise ordering of the stages, the idea that countries engage in an evolutionary and incremental mode of defence industrialisation is broadly accepted (see Table 1 below).[25]

**Table 1** The ladder of production in second-tier defence industrialisation

**Model 1**
1. Overhaul and service of imported weapons
2. Licensed assembly of foreign weapons
3. Manufacture of less complex components, with option of local final assembly
4. Increasing local design and manufacture of components, with local final assembly
5. Independent R&D and production

*Source*: James Everett Katz, *Arms Production in Developing Countries* (Lexington, MA: Lexington Books, 1984), p. 9.

**Model 2**
1. Initial import of arms from foreign suppliers
2. Maintenance and overhaul of imported weapons, including the manufacture of spare parts
3. Local assembly of imported subassemblies
4. Limited local component manufacturing; local licensed assembly
5. Some indigenous design and production, but important components imported
6. Local licensed production of less-advanced arms
7. Local licensed production for most weapons; limited indigenous R&D and production of less-advanced weapons
8. Indigenous design, development and production of weapon systems

*Source*: Janne E. Nolan, *Military Industry in Taiwan and South Korea* (New York: St. Martin's Press, 1986), pp. 45–46.

## Model 3

1.  Capability to perform simple maintenance
2.  Overhaul, refurbishment and rudimentary modification capabilities
3.  Assembly of imported components, simple licensed production
4.  Local production of components or raw materials
5.  Final assembly of less sophisticated weapons; some local component production
6.  Co-production or complete licensed production of less sophisticated weapons
7.  Limited R&D improvements to local licensed-produced arms
8.  Limited independent production of less sophisticated weapons; limited production [with foreign assistance] of more sophisticated weapons
9.  Independent R&D and production of less sophisticated weapons
10. Independent R&D and production of advanced arms with foreign components
11. Completely independent R&D and production

*Source*: Keith Krause, *Arms and the State: Patterns of Military Production and Trade* (Cambridge: Cambridge University Press, 1992), p. 170.

## Model 4

1.  Servicing and repair of imported weapon systems
2.  Overhaul of imported weapon systems
3.  Local assembly of imported subassemblies
4.  Limited licensed production; assembly with some locally-made components; locally made components sold to licenser
5.  Some independent licensed production, but important components are imported
6.  Local licensed production of less-advanced arms; R&D on improvements and derivatives
7.  Local licensed production for most weapons; limited R&D for advanced arms; R&D and production for less advanced arms
8.  Complete independence in R&D and production

*Source*: Michael J. Green, *Arming Japan: Defense Production, Alliance Politics, and the Postwar Search for Autonomy* (New York: Columbia University Press, 1995), p. 15.

According to the ladder of production, indigenous arms production is a process of transition from extremely high to very low levels of dependency on foreign sources of weapons and production technologies. Initial armaments production tends to rely heavily on imported technical assistance from countries possessing advanced defence industries. Most second-tier arms-producing countries start out by assembling weapon systems from imported parts and components (knock-down kits). The next step usually consists of the licensed production of foreign weapon systems, with some (and, in many cases, eventually nearly all) the actual manufacturing of components and subsystems performed indigenously. This is usually followed by limited indigenous development and production of relatively simple armaments, such as small arms, ordnance or small patrol boats, along with the development of more sophisticated armaments in partnership with more advanced foreign arms producers. Particularly at these later stages, basic arms-manufacturing capabilities are increasingly supplemented by incremental improvements in the country's independent military R&D. Accordingly, a country may attempt to indigenously produce more complex weapon systems, such as light armoured vehicles or trainer aircraft. Lastly, a country may attempt to design and develop its own advanced weapon systems, such as fighter aircraft, missiles, submarines, large surface combatants or military electronics, either across-the-board or by carving out certain niches or specialities.

This process has been repeated over and over again in the case of the second-tier arms-producing states. Before the late 1960s, few developing or newly industrialised countries possessed any arms industries to speak of. From humble beginnings countries such as Brazil, South Africa and Taiwan built up some of the most impressive defence industrial bases in the developing world. In most of these countries, military manufacturing initially centred around the production of such basic items as uniforms, automatic rifles, ammunition, grenades, mortars and mines. During the 1960s and 1970s, these countries also established aerospace industries, but these were mostly confined to licensed production of foreign combat aircraft. Brazil and South Africa, for example, both assembled versions of the Italian MB-326 light jet trainer, while Taiwan produced the US-designed F-5 fighter.

## Brazil

By the late 1980s, a number of second-tier arms-producing countries had made considerable progress in indigenising arms production. Brazil's Embraer, founded in 1969 with less than 600 workers, had by 1989 become the fifth-largest aircraft manufacturer in the world, with sales exceeding $700m – of which 70% was derived from exports – and a workforce totalling around 7,000 employees.[26] Embraer has developed the successful *Tucano* turboprop primary trainer aircraft, of which more than 600 have been sold to ten air forces around the world, including France and the UK.[27] With Italy, Embraer has also co-developed the AMX attack jet. The AMX boasts a fly-by-wire rudder-control system, advanced cockpit displays and two internal bays that can hold a variety of modular, 'plug-in' avionics. The Brazilian and Italian air forces have both purchased the AMX, which has also been exported to Venezuela. Other locally-produced military aircraft include the *Bandeirante* and *Brasilia* light transport planes.

During the 1970s and 1980s, Brazil emerged as a major producer of wheeled armoured vehicles and rocket artillery systems. Engesa (*Engenheiros Especializados SA*) built the EE-3 *Jararaca* scout car, the EE-9 *Cascavel* armoured car and the EE-11 *Urutu* armoured personnel carrier. On average, Engesa exported around 90% of its output, and the company sold its armoured vehicles to more than 20 countries, including Iraq, Libya, Colombia and Chile. Another Brazilian firm, Avibras, began producing the ASTROS (Artillery Saturation Rocket Bombardment System) multiple rocket launcher. Like Engesa, overseas sales accounted for nearly all of Avibras' revenues during the 1980s. The ASTROS was exported to Saudi Arabia, Iraq and Libya. In the 1980s, Engesa expanded into tracked vehicles, developing the EE-30 *Osorio* main battle tank, while Avibras designed a 300 kilometre-range ballistic missile, and reportedly even began work on a 1,000km-range missile. In addition, led by Orbita (an Engesa/Embraer joint venture), Brazil began several tactical-missile programmes, including the MAA-1 short-range air-to-air missile (AAM) , the MSA-3.1 shoulder-launched surface-to-air missile (SAM) and the MSS-1.2 anti-tank guided weapon.

## South Africa

By the late 1980s, South Africa had established an extensive and quite sophisticated arms industry, dominated by the state-owned Armscor. Beginning with the Italian MB-326 trainer jet (dubbed the

*Impala* by the South Africans), Armscor progressed from the assembly of imported kits to producing more than 90% of the aircraft indigenously. The company also modified the *Impala* design as a single-seat ground-attack version.[28] During the 1980s, Armscor undertook a major modification and upgrade of its fleet of French-built *Mirage* III fighter jets. About 50% of the existing *Mirage* III airframe was reconstructed, including an extended nosecone and the addition of canards (foreplanes) for improved agility. The fighter – renamed the *Cheetah* – was also given a new radar and avionics suite.[29] Armscor also developed the *Rooivalk* attack helicopter (currently in production for the South African armed forces), and during the 1980s even began preliminary work on a wholly indigenous fighter/ground-attack aircraft, designated the *Cava*.

The South African arms industry developed several weapons systems tailored for long-range desert and *veld* warfare.[30] During the 1970s, Armscor developed the G-5 towed howitzer which, along with its G-6 self-propelled cousin, is considered to be one of the most advanced artillery systems in the world.[31] The G-5 was exported to Iraq and used during the 1991 Gulf War. In addition, South Africa has built several types of military vehicles, including the *Eland* armoured car, the *Ratel* wheeled infantry fighting vehicle and the *Rooikat* scout vehicle, as well as UAVs.

South Africa also established a sizeable missile industry, building up particular expertise in air-to-air and air-to-surface missiles. Current missile systems include the V3C *Darter* AAM, the Multipurpose Stand-off Weapon (MUPSOW), the *Torgos* air-to-surface missile (ASM) and the *Mokopa* anti-tank guided munition.[32] The *Darter*, which can be mated with a state-of-the-art helmet-mounted sight and cueing system, is considered to be one of the most advanced short-range infrared-guided AAMs currently in production. A radar-guided, mid-range version of the *Darter* was unveiled at the 2001 Paris Air Show.

### South Korea

By the late 1980s, South Korea was self-sufficient in several areas of arms production. The country produces its own assault rifle for its armed forces, and is largely self-sufficient in items such as ammunition and artillery shells. It has also manufactured its own main battle tank (the K-1) and armoured vehicles (the KIFV infantry fighting vehicle). Other indigenous arms programmes include the KDX destroyer, the *Chun Ma* (*Pegasus*) SAM, the NHK-1 short-range ballistic missile and the K-9 self-propelled howitzer.

Seoul has focused particular attention on upgrading and 'indigenising' its aviation industry, and in the 1980s it launched an ambitious plan to place its aerospace industry among the world's top ten by 2005.[33] The first phase of the programme was the licensed-production of 120 F-16 fighters in the early 1990s, which entailed the establishment of a complete manufacturing facility in South Korea. Around the same time, South Korea also began work on two indigenous military aircraft projects, the KT-1 turboprop trainer and the KTX-2 supersonic trainer/light attack jet. The KT-1 programme was launched in the early 1990s, and entered production in 1999. The KTX-2 (since renamed the T-50) is a joint venture with Lockheed Martin, and is intended to replace advanced trainer jets and light fighter aircraft such as the T-38 and the F-5 in the South Korean Air Force, as well as being built for export. The T-50 is currently in full-scale development, at a cost of $2.1 billion; first flight took place in August 2002, and deliveries to the South Korean Air Force will begin in late 2005.[34]

This development plan also called for two other indigenous aircraft programmes, the FXX and the FXXX. The FXX involved the co-development of an advanced-technology multi-role fighter, via the upgrading of an existing Western aircraft such as the F-16 or the F/A-18. This would be followed by the FXXX, a fighter jet based on an entirely indigenous South Korean design. This programme was scheduled to start by the middle of the first decade of the twenty-first century.[35]

## Taiwan

For a small, newly industrialised economy, Taiwan has made considerable strides in indigenous arms production. It has particularly emphasised the establishment of a tactical missile industry, based in the Chung Shan Institute for Science and Technology (CSIST), located outside Taipei and owned and operated by the Ministry of National Defence. In the early 1980s, CSIST began producing the *Hsiung Feng* (*Male Bee*) anti-ship cruise missile (ASCM), reportedly a licensed-produced version of the Israeli *Gabriel* ASCM. The indigenously developed *Hsiung Feng* II ASCM – powered by a turbojet for increased range – followed in the mid-1990s. Both ramjet-powered (supersonic) and land-attack versions of the *Hsiung Feng* II are also reportedly under development.[36]

CSIST has also developed two AAM systems: the short-range *Tien Chien* I (*Sky Sword*), which is similar to the US AIM-9 *Sidewinder*, and the medium-range *Tien Chien* II, which is reportedly a fully active radar-homing AAM in the same class as the US-made AMRAAM. The *Tien Chien* I has been operational since the early 1990s, while the *Tien Chien* II entered production in the late 1990s. Variants of these systems include a surface-to-air version of the *Tien Chien* I and an anti-radiation version of the *Tien Chien* II, designed to attack ground-based air-defence radars.[37] Other missile systems include the *Tien Kung* I and II (*Sky Bow*) SAMs, a multiple rocket launcher and a short-range ballistic missile (which has never been put into service).

Taiwan has put considerable resources into building up its military aircraft industry. In 1969, the government created the Aerospace Industry Development Corporation (AIDC), a state-owned company based in Taichung. During the 1980s, AIDC successfully developed and produced the TCH-1 basic trainer and the AT-3 advanced trainer/light attack jet, building a total of 116 of these aircraft (52 TCH-1s and 64 AT-3s) for the Taiwanese Air Force. The centrepiece of recent AIDC production has been the IDF, a light, all-weather air-defence fighter similar in appearance and mission to the F-16. The IDF is outfitted with a multimode pulse-doppler radar, featuring both air- and sea-search modes and a look-down/shoot-down capability, and it can carry both air-to-air and air-to-surface missiles. With the IDF, Taiwan is actually one of the few second-tier arms producers to have designed, developed and manufactured its own supersonic fighter aircraft. The first prototype flew in May 1989, and the aircraft entered series production in 1994; a total of 130 were built between 1994 and 2000.

## Sweden

Rare among most second-tier arms producers, the roots of Sweden's arms industry date to the seventeenth century, with the establishment of companies such as Bofors (ordnance) and Karlskronavarvet (shipbuilding). The country's aerospace industry predates the Second World War, with the founding of Saab in 1937. Even so, until the 1940s Sweden still relied heavily on the licensed production of foreign armaments, including combat aircraft (from the US and Germany) and tanks (from Czechoslovakia). However, wartime cutoffs of armaments – reinforced by the advent of the Cold War – convinced the Swedes that they must be as self-sufficient as possible in arms procurement, which in turn impelled them to enlarge and improve their capabilities to design, develop and manufacture their own weapons.[38] Saab has long been the Swedish Air Force's primary source of combat aircraft, supplying fighters such as the J-29 *Tunnan*, the J-35 *Draken*, the AJ-37 *Viggen* and the present-day JAS-39 *Gripen*. Sweden has also developed and produced its own anti-ship cruise missiles (including the turbojet-powered RBS-15), armoured vehicles (such as the CV-90 infantry fighting vehicle and the unique S-103 turretless tank), artillery systems, surface-to-air and air-to-surface missiles, submarines and surface combatants.

Despite its small size and modest R&D budget, the Swedish defence industry has been adept at turning out sophisticated, state-of-the-art equipment. The J-21R fighter, introduced in the late 1940s, was one of Europe's first jet-powered combat aircraft, while the J-29 was one of the first swept-wing jet fighters to be introduced into service in a European air force. The J-35 was one of the earliest supersonic delta-wing fighters, while the *Viggen* pioneered several developments in combat aircraft design, including a canard/wing configuration, an onboard computer and a multimode pulse-doppler radar. In 1997, the *Gripen* was the first 'fourth-generation-plus' fighter to enter service. It incorporates a computerised delta wing/canard flight-control system for extreme agility, and the extensive use of composites and advanced avionics.[39] Sweden has also made considerable advances in low-observable technologies, in particular in the design and construction of 'stealthy' surface ships; was the first country in the world to deploy air-independent propulsion (AIP) in diesel-electric submarines; and was the first nation to produce a top-attack anti-tank missile designed to defeat reactive armour. Sweden possesses world-class capabilities in precision-guided weapons (terminally guided mortar rounds and smart artillery projectiles), radar (including airborne early-warning systems), defence electronics and communications and counter-mine warfare.

## The not-so-invisible hand: the indispensable role of the state in defence industrialisation

In nearly every second-tier case, the state has played an instrumental role in the establishment and nurturing of domestic arms industries, particularly in the case of developing and newly industrialised countries. In many instances, arms production has been either wholly or partly dominated by the state, often through military-run or state-owned enterprises such as AIDC, Embraer, IAI, Armscor and the Singapore Technologies Group. Even where arms production has remained largely in the hands of the private sector – as in Japan, Sweden and South Korea – state intervention in support of defence industrialisation has been instrumental.[40] In South Korea, for example, the government encouraged firms to enter into arms production through incentives such as tax breaks, low-interest loans and direct subsidies, and through coercive measures such as tying defence contracting to state support for other types of commercial production.[41]

In addition, the state has often assumed much of the risk for weapons development and production by mandating and funding an indigenous solution for a military hardware requirement. This strategy is particularly pronounced in the case of the second-tier countries' aerospace industries, where the bulk of production has traditionally been directed towards meeting domestic defence requirements, rather than commercial production.[42] Most of Taiwan's recent aviation-industry activity, for example, has centred on producing the IDF for the country's air force, while typically 75% to 80% of Japan's aircraft manufacturing is dependent on domestic defence contracts. Sweden and Israel have both aggressively pursued 'buy national' defence-procurement policies that underwrote local arms programmes and guaranteed large production runs.[43]

## Reality sets in: the second-tier arms producers in the post-Cold War era

Second-tier arms producers build weapons for many reasons: to possess an indigenous and therefore secure source of armaments; to promote industrial and technological development; to save or to make money; and for reasons of pride and prestige. As a result, Sweden during the Second World War, China in the 1950s, Brazil and South Africa in the 1960s and South Korea and Taiwan in the 1970s launched ambitious defence-industrialisation programmes, relying more or less on the evolutionary/incrementalist ladder-of-production model. To a large degree, these countries succeeded in creating sizeable, often impressive domestic arms industries. Certainly Sweden and Japan attained a level of technological sophistication and breadth in arms production equal to that of most first-tier states. In addition, many developing and newly industrialised countries – particularly Brazil, Israel, Singapore, South Africa and Taiwan – made remarkable progress in regard to a number of indigenous weapon systems; some were even able to carve out lucrative niches for themselves in the global arms marketplace.

Nevertheless, by the early 1990s the ladder-of-production model had shown itself to be a failure, and the second-tier states have ultimately failed to meet their most important objectives for indigenous arms production. In particular, they have not been able to achieve either autarky – that is, self-reliance in weapons design and technology – or efficiency – that is, making arms manufacturing cost-effective or deriving much in the way of economic benefits. More important, advanced arms production among second-tier states has become increasingly unsustainable. As the input demands of indigenous arms manufacturing – both in terms of financial resources and technology – escalate, these states find themselves increasingly hard-pressed to maintain even their current capacities and capabilities.

While many second-tier arms producers developed a capacity to produce finished weapon systems, they were unable to eliminate or even substantially reduce their reliance on foreign suppliers in several critical areas, particularly weapons design, engineering and development assistance, critical components and subsystems, machine tools and production know-how. For example:

- Brazil's highly successful *Tucano* military trainer aircraft incorporates several imported components – including the engine, landing gear and avionics. Ironically, many of Brazil's most ambitious indigenous arms programmes only increased the country's dependence on foreign military technologies and components. Seventy percent of the AMX fighter aircraft is imported, for instance, while the *Osorio* tank utilised a British suspension system and a German-designed engine and transmission.[44] In addition, weapon systems such as the MAA-1 missile and the SNAC-class submarine rely heavily on technical assistance, subsystems and even designs provided by Italy, the UK and Germany.

- Most of South Africa's so-called indigenous weapon systems are actually little more than reverse-engineered or updated versions of foreign weaponry. Self-sufficiency has mainly meant adapting and modifying existing foreign designs and technologies – what one analyst has referred to as 'add-on' (upgrading) or 'add-up' (cobbling together) engineering.[45] The *Cheetah* programme, for example, was essentially an upgrade of existing *Mirage* III airframes, while the indigenous *Rooivalk* attack helicopter was derived from the French-built SA-330 *Puma*.[46] At the same time, Israeli and Western European technical inputs have remained crucial to many South African weapons programmes. Israel, for example, reportedly provided critical assistance on the *Cheetah*, as well as aiding South Africa in the development of a radar-guided medium-range AAM, based on the Israeli *Python*.[47]

- South Korea's arms industry is only truly self-sufficient in small arms, ammunition and armoured vehicles; in most other cases, at least 40% of the value of 'indigenous production' is foreign in origin.[48] The T-50 advanced jet fighter, for example, depends heavily on technical assistance from Lockheed Martin, which is providing the plane's wing, computerised flight-control system and avionics; in fact, 55% of the T-50 will be produced in the US.[49] The K-1 tank was developed with 'substantial assistance' from General Dynamics; critical components such as the engine, transmission, gun and gunsight are imported from the US and Western Europe.[50] The *Chun Ma* SAM utilises a French-built missile and fire-control system, while the KIFV infantry fighting vehicle is essentially a reverse-engineered copy of a US-designed vehicle, incorporating a licensed-produced German engine and British transmission.[51]

- Sweden has actually increased its dependence upon imported weapon systems, subsystems and military technologies. The *Gripen*, for example, utilises significantly more imported components and technology than any previous Swedish military programme; up to 40% of the JAS-39 is foreign-sourced, compared to 20% for the *Viggen*.[52] Moreover, in the early 1990s the Swedish army chose to buy and license-produce the German *Leopard* II main battle tank over a domestic design, citing unaffordable development costs. Stockholm will also procure its artillery systems from foreign suppliers, and co-develop its next generation of submarines.

- Taiwan's IDF is almost anything but: airframe design and development was overseen by Lockheed Martin; the engine is simply an upgraded version of Allied Signal's TFE-731 turbofan; and the radar was derived from the General Electric APG-67 radar originally developed for the F-20 fighter.

Except for a few exceptional cases, such as Sweden or Japan, defence industrialisation has failed to help second-tier arms producers attain an advanced level of *independent* military-technological innovation and development. Most typically possess limited or underdeveloped defence R&D bases, and they tend to suffer from shortages of skilled personnel and lack the scientific and technical infrastructures to pursue breakthroughs and applied research in many critical technologies. Consequently, many second-tier arms producers – particularly those in the developing world but also in many rapidly industrialising states as well – remain deficient in indigenous capacities for design, engineering and manufacture. These deficiencies include arcane military technologies (such as very low observability), militarily critical supporting technologies (such as propulsion, advanced materials, space-based assets, sensors, guidance systems, aerodynamics, information technologies and microelectronics) and advanced manufacturing technologies (such as computer-assisted design and manufacturing (CAD/CAM), advanced fabrication techniques or 'lean' manufacturing).[53]

In addition, most second-tier arms-producing countries lack sufficient funding to support a broad-based, self-sustaining defence technology base. Typically, these countries have allocated few resources to military R&D: South Korea during the 1990s spent less than $500m annually on R&D; Taiwan spent only around $300m and South Africa around $100m.[54] Swedish defence R&D budgets have dropped dramatically, from $520m in 1995 to $140m in 1998.[55]

The end of the Cold War has only exacerbated many of these resource constraints. Stockholm, arguing that 'an invasion attempt aiming at the occupation of Sweden does not seem feasible in the coming ten years', aims to reduce military expenditures by 10% by 2004; more significantly, annual procurement spending will be cut by one-third over the next decade.[56] In South Africa, the end of apartheid and the transition to democracy, along with military withdrawals from Angola, Namibia and Mozambique, have resulted in dramatic disarmament and defence cuts. Military spending has declined by more than half since 1989; more importantly, military R&D spending has fallen by at least 65%, while procurement spending has dropped by more than 80%.[57] Japan has also cut R&D and procurement budgets, as domestic economic troubles have caused military spending to stagnate.[58]

With the possible exception of a few advanced industrialised countries such as Sweden and Japan, therefore, there still exists a sizeable and fixed 'technology lag' between the first- and second-tier states.[59] Few second-tier arms producers can lay claim to significant military-technology breakthroughs. Rather, innovation remains 'firmly anchored in the industrialized countries', who continue to dominate the frontiers of armaments development, further eroding the efforts of second-tier states to stay technologically competitive.[60] Among developing countries such as Brazil, South Africa, South Korea and Taiwan, their best home-grown military equipment is still relatively simple in design and construction: small arms and munitions, artillery pieces, armoured vehicles and trainer aircraft. Other indigenous military systems – such as combat aircraft, missiles, or night-vision equipment – are at least a generation behind those produced by the first-tier states (and which are, incidentally, increasingly available on the global arms market).[61]

Moreover, there are few 'latecomer' advantages to being an arms producer – that is, the ability to leverage technological breakthroughs pioneered by others and to incorporate these into indigenous products at a lower cost and in less time. Compared with other industrial sectors, such as electronics and car manufacturing, the barriers to entry into the global arms business are high. First, technology transfer – the most widely-used process for establishing industries in new locations – is much more tightly controlled than in most commercial manufacturing sectors. The most diffused military-related *design* and *development* technologies (as opposed to manufacturing technologies) – such as those concering small arms and munitions – are generally 'mature' ones, or at least not state-of-the-art. At the same time, first-tier arms markets are generally closed, eliminating the low-wage advantage that many developing or newly industrialised countries bring to various commercial sectors, such as automobiles, consumer electronics, toys and clothing, when selling to large markets in the industrialised world.[62]

In general, arms production in many second-tier states is often inefficient and poorly run. In many Asian and developing countries, for example, industrial management styles tend to be rigidly hierarchical, bureaucratic and risk-averse. Linkages between producer and customer (i.e., the local military) are poor, and quality control is often lacking. In addition, the predilection of many governments for high-technology 'prestige projects', such as combat aircraft and missile systems, and an over-confidence in their industries' abilities to quickly move such programmes into production, has often resulted in unexpected development problems, delays, cost overruns and failure.[63] Overall, most second-tier arms producers are:

> *not technologically mature and sophisticated enough to pursue ... independent defense industrialization. Such a strategy is even more technologically demanding as [these states] must begin to advance beyond the [areas of] conventional weapons production in which [they are] gradually losing competitive advantage.[64]*

As a result, these countries' defence industries remain highly exposed to global forces controlling the diffusion of military technology, and for most second-tier states the goal of autarky in arms production – or even a greater degree of self-sufficiency than at present – is a rapidly receding dream. In sum, self-reliance has been largely reduced to a shibboleth – a catchphrase to mask the fact that second-tier arms-producing states have simply replaced one form of dependency (finished weapon systems) with another (critical military technologies and subsystems).

Arms production has also brought few macroeconomic benefits. First, weapons manufacturing is often an 'enclave industrial activity', making little overall contribution to a country's economic progress. Anticipated spin-off or economic multiplier benefits – such as expanded resource utilisation, commercially useful spin-off technologies and workforce education and training – usually do not manifest themselves in large enough quantities to be worthwhile.[65] Rather, there are continuing opportunity costs to arms production, as countries must constantly invest and innovate in order to remain globally competitive in military technology. Overall, therefore, there are few permanent industrial-developmental advantages accruing to indigenous arms production.

Moreover, second-tier arms manufacturing is rarely cost-effective. Arms production in these countries is typically geared towards meeting domestic requirements, which in turn usually means small, inefficient production runs and high unit costs.[66] Development costs for Japan's F-2 fighter, for example, have more than doubled since the programme began, and final costs are estimated at around $100m per plane – at least three times the cost of the F-16 aircraft upon which it is based. The F-2's development phase has also doubled in length, further adding to programme costs.[67] In South Korea's case, Seoul's insistence on producing the F-16 indigenously added about 20%, or $1 billion, to the cost of procurement; earlier efforts to licence-produce the F-5 fighter and MD-500 helicopter added similar cost surpluses, yet these programmes reportedly transferred little by way of advanced technology.[68] Both Brazil's AMX subsonic strike fighter and South Korea's T-50 advanced trainer/light attack jet cost nearly as much as an F-16, and yet neither matches the F-16 in performance.[69] In fact, in many second-tier states it is increasingly difficult to justify arms production from a profit point of view. As a result, most defence-industrial sectors – particularly aerospace – depend heavily upon subsidies and protection provided by the central government, which often runs these as 'prestige' industries.[70]

Excess production capacity has further eroded cost-effective arms production. Beginning in the early 1980s, many second-tier states greatly expanded their arms-manufacturing capacities in response to existing or projected needs, only to find themselves saddled with too many workers and under-utilised, high-overhead facilities when these programmes never materialised or else were terminated prematurely. During the 1980s, Brazil, Israel and South Africa had each begun work on building their own fighter aircraft; none of these projects ever made it out of development. In addition:

- South Korean aerospace firms invested billions of dollars in new factories and advanced machine tools, not only to licence-produce the F-16 fighter but also in response to ambitious national plans to establish the country as one of the top ten aerospace producers by around the turn of the century. These plans included South Korea building an entirely indigenous fighter by 2010, as well as a 100-seat regional jet.[71] In fact, neither of these projects ever came to fruition, and as a result the South Korean aviation industry currently operates at only 30% of capacity, is more than $1bn in debt, and continues to haemorrhage money.[72]

- Taiwan's AIDC built a modern production facility to undertake an expected production run of 250 IDFs. With the 1992 purchase of 150 F-16s and 60 French *Mirage*-2000s, however, IDF procurement was subsequently cut back to 130, the last of which was delivered in January 2000. Consequently, AIDC factories are taken up with 'idle assembly lines' and 'large rooms filled with little-used machines'.[73] The state-owned China Shipbuilding Corporation (CSC), which builds most of Taiwan's warships, is similarly plagued by low worker productivity and heavy debts.

- In the late 1980s, Brazil's defence industries attempted to build on their earlier export successes by expanding into new product areas, such as main battle tanks, jet fighters and anti-ship and ballistic missiles, but few of these programmes ever made it into production. Engesa, for example, spent $100m of its own money on the *Osorio* tank programme, but failed to secure any domestic or foreign orders.[74] So far, Brazil has sold only 12 AMX aircraft to a single foreign customer (Venezuela), while domestic orders for the AMX have been cut from 100 to 70 aircraft.

Overlapping investments and excess competition have exacerbated over-capacity and poor economies of scale. By the early 1990s, for example, South Korea boasted three separate aircraft companies, despite a lack of work. That, however, did not prevent the Hyundai conglomerate from buying a small aircraft company and then investing $1bn in a new factory in an attempt to break into the aerospace business.[75] In Japan, three companies build aircraft and, until recently, two firms in Sweden produced missiles. During the 1960s and 1970s, Beijing established redundant centres of armaments production in the remote interior of southern and western China – the so-called 'Third Line' – to protect the country's strategic industries from being overrun or destroyed in the event of a Soviet invasion. Approximately 55% of China's defence industries are located within the Third Line, yet most of these industries are losing money – requiring continued infusions of state funds – as well as being much less productive than firms located in coastal areas.[76]

The winding down of several major regional conflicts at the end of the 1980s – and the subsequent slowdown in Third World defence spending and arms purchases – was ruinous for many export-dependent second-tier arms producers. In the case of Brazil, for example, the end of the Iran–Iraq War in 1988 (Baghdad was Brazil's single largest customer at the time) contributed to a significant decline in Brazilian arms exports, from $874m in 1988 to $144m in 1989, and then to $69m in 1990.[77]

At the same time, it has become more economical in the post-Cold War era to purchase foreign weapons than to develop and produce arms indigenously. Given global over-capacities in armaments production and an international arms market that is only one-third as large as in the late 1980s, the subsequent buyer's market for arms has undermined some of the strongest arguments for indigenous production. With suppliers competing with each other to sell in a tightening market, access to some of the world's most advanced arms is hardly a problem. At the same time, sellers have been quick to offer competitive prices and other economic incentives, such as low-cost financing and industrial offsets. As a result, buyers can often acquire foreign weapons that are both superior and less expensive than domestically sourced ones.

Overall, despite expectations of industrial benefits, arms production rarely contributes much to a country's economic development, particularly when it comes to directly stimulating the growth of critical high-technology industries, such as microelectronics and computing, telecommunications, automobiles or ship-building (one possible exception might be the aviation sector – but even then, much of the basis for this industry remains import-dependent). Rather, a well-developed industrial infrastructure is usually an essential prerequisite for a successful arms-production capability. In his investigation of over 30 developing countries, Jurgen Brauer found that:

> *Even if [non-arms-producing developing countries] had politico-military incentives to produce arms indigenously, in general they do not possess the industrial and human capital to do so …[while] among [developing nations who do produce arms], one observes a close correspondence between potential for arms production and actual arms production; i.e., the*

*more developed the industrial structure, the more arms [these countries produce.*[78]

Brauer concluded that 'the effective sufficiency argument for arms production by developing nations is economic ability, not politico-military incentive'.[79] In other words, it is pre-existing industrial capacities that stimulate and permit arms production, and not the other way around. A state, of course, may make a conscious effort to create the necessary economic and industrial conditions for arms manufacturing and thus help lay the groundwork for defence industrialisation, but arms production can hardly be considered the driver of industrial development.[80]

## Facing up to the learning curve

Arms production is a capital- and technology-intensive industry requiring significant investments in equipment and personnel.[81] Increasingly, second-tier arms-producing states lack both the financial resources and the technology – which can be regarded as a subset of wealth – to advance indigenous defence industrialisation.

As a result, most of these countries – especially those in the developing world – have levelled off at an intermediate stage of technology, both when it comes to the *types* of weapon systems they can produce indigenously and to their *capacities* for production (i.e., independent design and development).[82] Despite national security imperatives and political-military inducements pressing them onwards, these countries find themselves in the middle of the ladder of production and increasingly hard-pressed to move further up.[83] As Keith Krause has put it, most second-tier producer-countries have been stranded on a 'technology plateau', where they are either 'unable to ascend to higher levels of production' or even find themselves 'regress[ing] to lower rungs on the ladder' of production.[84]

Ultimately, there are several flaws in the incrementalist/ evolutionary ladder-of-production model of defence industrialisation. First, it is often overly deterministic, which can lead to an expectation of inevitable linear progress. A country entering into armaments production might assume from this model that advancement up the ladder is somehow predetermined and 'natural'. James Katz has described the ladder of production as 'a "natural history" in the actualization of a weapons-system production program'.[85] Yet, as

Susan Willett has observed, the process of defence industrialisation 'is seldom linear or incremental – it may often acquire a non-linear, dynamic quality'.[86] Progress is likely to be fitful and erratic, and performance can vary widely. Willett adds that:

> *In reality, progress through the various stages is not necessarily uniform; the progress of arms industries in some developing countries has omitted several stages or ... [fallen back] following an over-ambitious program ... While a few countries may be further up the ladder in terms of some weapons categories, such as armored vehicles, naval ships, and submarines, they may be near the bottom in other categories, such as missiles and aircraft.[87]*

Furthermore, it is often assumed that there is a learning curve built into this model. In a perfect world, of course, an arms producer would hope that each input of resources would result in the same measure of output in the form of autarky as the player progressed up the ladder of production. Hence, as Figure 1 shows, the cost of going from A to B (i.e., from complete dependency to partial autarky) would be roughly the same as advancing from B to C and from C to D (i.e., from partial to near-total autarky). In the real world, however, there tend to be quite significant start-up costs to arms production, as laboratories and research facilities must be established, factories must be built, machinery purchased and scientists, technicians and workers trained. Nevertheless, nations entering into arms production may do so with the assumption that they can build upon initial infrastructure investments, learning and experiences in order to achieve cost-efficiencies later on in the arms-production process. Therefore, a country may expect the autarky-versus-efficiency (efficiency expressed in terms of resource outlays) ratio to actually improve as its defence industry progresses up the ladder of production. As Figure 2 demonstrates, while there are higher costs for each output of autarky at the lower rungs of the ladder of production (curve AB), it is conceivable that these costs would flatten out after a while (curve BCD). There is a logic to this argument: certain capital outlays, such as factory construction and the purchase of machine tools, can be paid off, and workforce skills and expertise should mature and improve. Moreover, as a country's

**Figure 1** The Ladder of Production

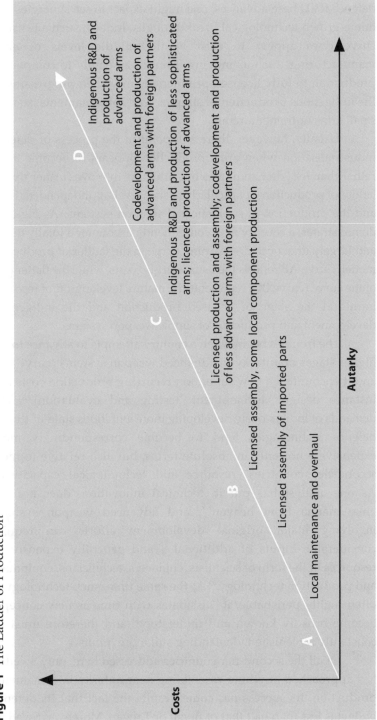

defence R&D base advances, one might expect to see synergies and home-grown technological breakthroughs. Indeed, such a learning curve does appear to exist at the middle levels of arms manufacturing, such as moving from kit assembly to component production to fully licensed production, and when progressing to the indigenous production of simpler types of armaments, such as small arms or trainer aircraft.

Usually, however, there is a point in the process of defence industrialisation when arms production appears to become *more*, rather than *less*, demanding as one attempts to move further up the ladder of production – particularly to such levels as independent R&D and the production of sophisticated weapon systems. As Figure 3 demonstrates, a country may consequently encounter a totally new – and largely unexpected – learning curve in the ladder of production model. Curve AB reflects the usual start-up costs, while the flatter part of the curve (curve BC) represents the mature levelling-off of resource inputs at the stage of licensed production and the indigenous development and production of simple weapon systems.

The troubles begin when a country attempts to advance to the higher stages of autarky in advanced weapon systems (curve CD) and it encounters a new set of non-recurring production costs (for instance design, development, testing and evaluation).[88] The demands of indigenously developing more ambitious state-of-the-art defence technologies tend to become correspondingly more expensive – not only in absolute terms, but also relative to most second-tier countries' resource and technological capacities.[89] As one analyst has put it, technical innovation 'does not fall "like manna from heaven"', and advanced weapon systems involving major original development efforts can require considerable inputs of additional – and generally expensive – resources in the form of scientists, engineers, technicians, equipment and production technology.[90] At the same time, such technology is often highly perishable; it 'dissipates with time as new concepts become broadly known and understood' and therefore must be constantly replenished, demanding still more inputs.[91]

Of all the second-tier countries addressed here, only Sweden has approached anything resembling near-autarky in armaments production. Its success has come despite the fact that its defence budget is less than half that of Brazil or Taiwan. Moreover, Swedish

**Figure 2** The Learning Curve

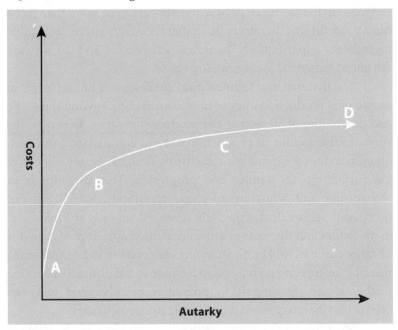

**Figure 3** The Double Learning Curve

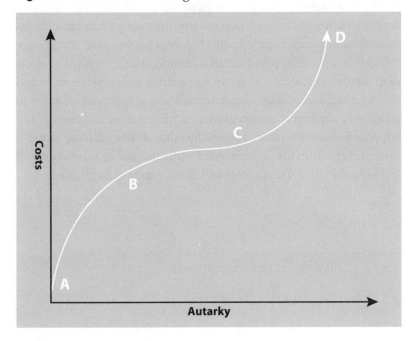

military spending has been more or less static for over 20 years.[92] Progress up the ladder of production appears to be more than just a matter of funds, therefore; it demands other, more intangible ingredients – particularly historical experience and an already advanced industrial and technology base.

The material and technological challenges of higher levels of armaments production appear to be increasingly beyond the scope and capabilities of all second-tier producer countries. In reality, the rungs in this ladder of production are not equidistant from each other, nor does weapons manufacturing necessarily get any easier the further up the ladder one progresses. The difficulty is in recognising and adjusting to these conditions, which are not necessarily self-evident, especially when a country is at a mid-level in the ladder and the costs of arms production appear moderate (for instance curve BC in Figure 3). In fact, successes in indigenous arms manufacturing early on may blind a nation to the difficulties lurking further ahead, causing it to pursue more advanced weapons production that may mean it outpacing its competencies.

Most second-tier arms producers were undone by 'technology overreach'. Particularly for countries such as Brazil, South Africa and South Korea, their earlier success lay largely in their ability to produce relatively simple, rugged and inexpensive military equipment. Ironically, such success was ultimately their undoing, as technonationalism, coupled with the impetus towards the greater indigenisation of supply, created a 'momentum ... toward projects of greater sophistication'.[93] At the same time, local producers lacked the funding, technology or economies and efficiencies of scale to effectively support these programmes.[94] Even more technologically advanced countries such as Japan, Sweden and Israel have found it increasingly difficult to keep pace with the rising economic and technological demands of state-of-the-art armaments production.

# Chapter 2

## Transition and Readjustment in Second-Tier Defence Industries: Five Case Studies

Second-tier arms producers face a dual dilemma: they tend to pay higher costs for less-capable indigenous weaponry, while at the same time they have not freed themselves of their dependencies on and subordination to first-tier arms producers in critical technologies and components. In particular, the traditional 'autarky-versus-efficiency' argument is increasingly irrelevant for the second-tier arms industries, since sustainable self-reliance is neither technologically feasible nor cost-effective, resulting in indigenous weapons that are often inferior to, as well as more expensive than, those readily found on the international arms market.

Many second-tier countries are candidly rethinking their long-term plans. The Swedish government, for example, has admitted that autarky is no longer 'economically and technically possible'.[1] In a 1998 white paper on defence-related industries, South Africa asserted that budgetary realities 'made it impossible to maintain all [of its] required technologies and capabilities within the broader South African industrial base'.[2] Taiwan has acknowledged that, since the 'purchase of weapons from foreign countries is easier than before ... the original plan for independent production of weapons must be stopped or reduced'.[3] Even South Korea – which still places a high priority on domestic procurement – has accepted that future arms acquisitions must be made 'more economical'.[4]

Second-tier states can pursue several transition and readjustment strategies. These include:

- **Quitting the defence business.** A country may choose simply to abandon all or some defence production, shutting down its unneeded arms factories and laying off or transferring redundant defence workers.

- **Rationalising and consolidating defence operations.** Alternatively, a country may decide to continue with defence work, but adjust its defence industry to meet harsher economic realities and lowered expectations. This generally entails privatising state-owned industries, reducing over-capacity and excess competition by shedding excess workers, closing down unneeded factories and encouraging mergers and acquisitions, and focusing on core operations and key competencies in niche products.

- **Diversification.** A country may choose to convert some of its arms-production capacity to non-military work. Defence plants may retool to produce civilian products, or else acquire new businesses.

- **Leveraging dual-use technologies for military production.** A country may attempt to bolster indigenous arms production by adapting dual-use civilian technologies to meet military needs, such as wireless and fibre-optic telecommunications for command and control systems, or computers for information processing.

- **Increasing arms exports.** Arms producers may attempt to compensate for reduced domestic defence demand by expanding overseas sales.

- **Globalisation.** Finally, a producer may choose to maintain and develop its defence industry by expanding its participation in international arms activities. Globalisation includes *ad hoc* teaming arrangements to co-develop or co-produce armaments, establishing international joint-venture companies, and cross-border mergers and acquisitions.[5]

None of these approaches is mutually exclusive, and a country may – and usually will – pursue several at the same time. Different countries may heavily favour one or two particular responses. On the other hand, there may be particular approaches that nearly all countries will undertake. This chapter compares and contrasts the various readjustment activities of several second-tier states as they wrestle with the problems of armaments production in the post-Cold War era.

## Brazil: painful exit, successful niche producer

In 1989, Brazil possessed one of the largest and most sophisticated arms industries in the developing world, and the country was a leading producer and exporter of military equipment. By the early 1990s, however, its defence industry all but disappeared. This collapse led to one of the few notable efforts by a second-tier state to dramatically retrench its arms-producing capacities. Statistics are unavailable, but it is reasonable to assume that, during the 1990s, overall defence-related employment in Brazil shrank by at least half. Moreover, Brazil's leadership in the early 1990s was largely prepared to let the defence industry go under – a rarity among governments in the developing world. The democratisation and demilitarisation of governance created a political environment that had little sympathy for the plight of arms-producing companies. In addition, poor economic conditions made it difficult to rescue failing industries, while political chaos translated into weak governments unable to take decisive action.[6]

Rapidly-falling export sales forced both Engesa and Avibras to lay off much of their workforce during 1988–89. Losses continued to mount, however, and Avibras declared bankruptcy in January 1990. Engesa followed suit the following March. Eventually, it closed down its entire armoured-vehicle production line and laid off over 3,000 employees.[7] At around the same time, the Orbita missile consortium – of which Engesa was a key partner – also collapsed into bankruptcy. The government subsequently transferred most of its programmes to a different company, Mectron Engenharia, but this has failed to prevent major setbacks in the missile industry. Of Orbita's three leading missile programmes, only the MAA-1 AAM is likely to enter production in the near future; the development of both the MSS-1.2 anti-tank missile and the MSA-3.1 SAM was largely suspended during the 1990s, and although still considered active, these programmes will probably never enter production.[8] Most other Brazilian missile programmes were simply terminated.

Avibras has maintained its defence business, albeit at a greatly curtailed level of activity. In fact, the company has experienced a modest comeback as an arms exporter, securing an order in early 2001 from Malaysia for 12 ASTROS multiple rocket launchers, worth $120m. For the most part, however, Avibras mainly services existing systems and sells replacement rockets.[9] Moreover, with its accession to the Missile Technology Control Regime (MTCR) in 1995, Brazil terminated Avibras' ballistic-missile programmes. The company continues to work on Brazil's VLS commercial space-launch vehicle, but the first two launches of this system, in November 1997 and December 1999, both failed.[10]

Naval shipbuilding has also been sharply reduced, and during the 1990s only one corvette and one submarine (the last Type-209) started construction. Brazil has reportedly resurrected plans to design and build its own class of diesel-powered and then nuclear-powered submarines. However, construction of the first in this class is unlikely to begin before 2003, for delivery in late 2008.[11]

Embraer was also hard-hit in the early 1990s. Weak international sales and heavy losses forced the company to lay off more than half of its workforce, or approximately 3,500 employees. A sharp downturn in the international aviation market only exacerbated Embraer's already precarious situation. After two attempts to denationalise the company failed, Embraer was finally sold off in December 1994 to a private consortium (the Brazilian government retained a 'golden share' (a controlling interest) in the company). Embraer's new management immediately restructured the company's debt, negotiating a 10% wage reduction and investing in new skills and training. In particular, the company concentrated on a new family of commercial aircraft, centring around the 50-seat ERJ-145 regional jet. The ERJ-145 entered production in 1996 and was an immediate success. By 2000, orders and options totalled more than 700 aircraft from 23 customers in 15 countries. Embraer produces two smaller versions of the ERJ-145, the 37-seat ERJ-135 (over 400 orders and options) and the 44-seat ERJ-140. The company also builds the EMB-120 *Brasilia* (a 30-seat turboprop), more than 350 of which have been delivered since the mid-1980s.[12] Other commercial activities include producing parts for the MD-11 and Boeing-747, -767, and -777 airliners, and for the Sikorsky S-92 helicopter. The company is currently developing a new line of aircraft, the 70-

passenger Embraer-170 and the 100-passenger Embraer-190. First deliveries of the Embraer-170 are expected in 2004, followed the Embraer-190 in 2005. Industry analysts expect the market for 70–100-seat regional jets to more than double by 2008, and Embraer could become a formidable competitor in this sector.[13] At the same time, Embraer has greatly scaled down its defence business, and military aircraft production accounts for less than 15% of overall revenues.

From a loss of $379m in 1994 Embraer turned a $109m profit in 1998 – its first in over a decade. Net profits in 1999 were $230m on record sales of $1.9bn; by 2001, Embraer's backlog of orders totalled more than $23bn.[14] In 1999, Embraer became Brazil's largest exporter, with overseas sales of more than $1.7bn. Altogether, exports account for nearly 90% of revenues, aided by export financing provided by the Brazilian government. Embraer expects overseas deliveries to reach $5bn annually by around 2005.[15] At the same time, worker productivity has risen dramatically. The time required to produce the ERJ-145 and the EMB-120 *Brasilia* has declined, while revenues per employee have jumped from $40,000 in 1994 to $252,000 in 1999. Employment in 2002 stood at more than 11,000 – surpassing pre-privatisation levels.[16]

Embraer's shrinking military aircraft division – after years without any new sales – is also making a small comeback. The company has developed the ALX light attack aircraft, based on the *Tucano* trainer, which it is currently producing for the Brazilian Air Force. The ALX can carry both air-to-air and air-to-ground weapons, and will also be qualified for night missions and as an intermediate trainer. The Air Force plans to buy 99 ALXs, to be produced between 2003 and 2006.[17] The ALX has been exported to the Dominican Republic, but a planned purchase by Colombia of up to 40 ALXs never came to fruition. Embraer also builds two militarised versions of the ERJ-145: the EMB-145SA, which is outfitted with the Swedish *Erieye* radar system for airborne surveillance and early warning; and the EMB-145S, which is intended for maritime patrol. The EMB-145SA has been sold to the Brazilian Air Force and the Greek armed forces.

Despite its successes, however, Embraer accepts that it cannot go it alone in the global aviation market. In fact, it is already a highly globalised and import-dependent company. For example, approximately 50% of the value of the ERJ-145 is imported, including the aircraft's engine, avionics and flight controls; fully 35% of the aircraft is composed of US-built parts. In addition, the company has actively solicited its foreign suppliers to become risk-sharing partners on its regional jet programmes, and therefore assume a percentage of the plane's development costs. The Embraer-170/-190 programme, for example, will be built in partnership with 16 companies from around the world, including Kawasaki of Japan, Latecoere of France and five US firms.[18] A similar risk-sharing arrangement is used to build the ERJ-145 regional jet.

Just as important, ever since its privatisation Embraer has sought to team up with a foreign company in the hope that this would expand its global reach as well as facilitate its access to foreign capital and technologies. In 1999, after investigating a possible tie-up with Britain's BAE Systems, Embraer sold a 20% share in the company to a consortium of four French aerospace firms, Aerospatiale Matra, Dassault Aviation, Snecma Motors and Thales.[19]

Overall, Brazil has largely left the defence business. It no longer produces armoured vehicles, its artillery rocket and military aircraft businesses have shrunk considerably while its missile industry was largely stillborn. Moreover, Brazil is no longer a major player in the international arms market; by the late 1990s, for example, its annual arms exports amounted to less than 10% of the average level in the 1980s. Despite some short-term pain, however, Brazil has largely recovered – due in large part to the country's general economic resurgence in the late 1990s.

Still, there are risks to Brazil's defence readjustment efforts, particularly for Embraer. The company continues to carry a heavy debt burden, and a ruling by the World Trade Organisation (WTO) that Brazil's aircraft-export financing programme constitutes an illegal subsidy could hurt future sales. In addition, weak sales in 2001 forced the company to institute layoffs – totalling nearly 15% of its workforce – for the first time since privatisation.[20] Finally, Embraer's jump into 70–100-passenger regional jets puts the company into a highly competitive new business sector. Overall, however, Brazil serves as an excellent example not only of the limitations of the defence industrialisation-led development model, but also of the economic successes possible through diversification away from defence production.

## South Africa: importing to preserve domestic arms industries

Few second-tier arms industries have been as hard-hit as South

Africa's, and few have pursued such radical and far-reaching readjustment. One of the first moves came in 1992 when, in an effort to commercialise the public-sector defence industry, the government restructured Armscor's arms-manufacturing units into a new parastatal (state-owned enterprise) called Denel. More than half of all South African arms production was concentrated in Denel, and it dominates the country's aerospace, missile, artillery and ordnance sectors. Under this new organisation, although the government held all of its shares, Denel was expected to operate as a private commercial enterprise, without public subsidies. In addition, ownership of Denel was transferred from the Defence Ministry to the Department of Public Enterprises, which is responsible for the eventual privatisation of all South African parastatals.

At the same time, Denel and other South African arms producers have lost most of their former status as protected and subsidised industries. Under pressure to become more cost-efficient and economically viable, these firms have engaged in a broad array of transition and readjustment strategies. Above all, the emphasis has shifted away from possessing the capacity to design, develop and manufacture a broad array of weapon systems to one based on leveraging so-called core competencies in defence products and services. In particular, the South African arms industry has laid out a number of niche programmes, including electronics, communications and sensors, UAVs and a few finished weapon systems – particularly wheeled vehicles, missiles and artillery and munitions.[21] The defence industry sees itself as capable of providing critical services as a systems integrator, both for domestic and foreign consumption. As weapon platforms become more modular, they will be increasingly comprised of 'open architectures' that can be adapted to utilise customised weapons packages and subsystems. South African defence firms – based on their longstanding niche expertise in the areas of add-on and add-up engineering – view themselves as particularly well-placed to function as systems designers and programme managers when it comes to adapting and upgrading weapon systems for new roles and missions.[22]

In addition, over the past decade the South African arms industry has experienced dramatic retrenchment and rationalisation. Between 1989 and 1998, the number of workers directly or indirectly employed in local arms manufacturing declined by more than 60%, from 130,000 to 50,000. Denel alone fell from 30,000 to 13,000 employees; it also laid off 40% of its scientists and engineers.[23] Two of the country's largest privately-owned arms producers, Reunert and Altech, although much less dependent on defence contracting than Denel, also suffered declines in employment.[24]

South Africa's defence industries have also attempted to strengthen their market base by expanding into commercial work.[25] Approximately one-fifth to one-quarter of Denel's revenues comes from non-military production, up from around 10% in the early 1990s.[26] South Africa's three largest private-sector arms producers – Reunert, Altech and Grintek – have also reduced their dependence on arms production, mainly through diversifying and divesting themselves of defence subsidiaries.[27] South Africa has also greatly increased arms exports over the past decade, from $33m in 1989 to $181m in 1999. Denel has sold its G-5 and G-6 155mm artillery systems to Oman, Malaysia and the United Arab Emirates (UAE), UAVs to Algeria and artillery propellants and laser range-finders to the UK. Reunert has sold mine-protected armoured vehicles to the UN and radios to Romania, Grintek has exported electronic warfare systems to Switzerland and the UAE and Altech developed a new navigation and attack system for Spanish Air Force *Mirage* F-1 fighters.[28] By 2000, overseas sales accounted for 35% of Denel's income.[29]

These efforts have had only mixed success, however. In particular, attempts to make Denel more financially self-sufficient have largely been unsuccessful. Since it was created, turnover has declined and profitability has been sporadic at best; the company lost millions of dollars during the 1990s and only turned a slight profit in 2001.[30] Moreover, some of Denel's most ambitious diversification programmes have been painful failures, particularly an attempt to break into the commercial satellite sector.[31] These setbacks have, in turn, delayed privatisation until at least 2004.[32]

Nor have arms exports been a reliable source of revenue. The defence industry is extremely dependent on sales to just a few countries – particularly Algeria, which accounted for over 70% of South Africa's overseas arms deals in 1998.[33] Efforts to sell some of South Africa's most advanced weapon systems – such as the *Rooivalk* attack helicopter – have generally met with little success. Finally, overseas arms sales have been constrained by a stringent export-control regime established by the post-apartheid government that prohibits arms exports to countries in conflict; this has cost the country sales to Turkey (due to its civil war with Kurdish separatists) and much of Sub-Saharan Africa. Consequently, the South African arms industry has established a rather modest goal of R800m to R1.2bn ($110m to $155m) a year – or approximately one-sixth of total defence-industry revenues – for future arms exports.[34]

Paradoxically, *importing* arms may do more to aid South Africa's defence industry than any home-grown endeavour. In September 1999, Pretoria signed agreements with several Western European firms to buy up to R30bn ($4.5bn)-worth of new weapons, including 28 *Gripen* fighter jets from Sweden, 24 *Hawk* advanced jet trainers from the UK, 30 light utility helicopters from Italy and four corvettes and three diesel-powered submarines from Germany. These purchases come with a package of offsets and industrial participation programmes worth up to R104bn ($15bn) over the next decade (2001–2011). This includes approximately $3bn in direct offsets to local arms producers – i.e., co-production, technology transfers and third-party export participation – $5bn in foreign investment in the South African defence industry and $6bn in indirect offsets (counter-purchases of South African products by foreign defence firms). Altogether, these offsets could create up to 65,000 defence and non-defence jobs, and as such were arguably the 'primary justification' for this arms purchase.[35]

Overall, offsets from this package deal could equal nearly 15% of the South African arms industry's total annual revenues for the next several years.[36] Denel alone could receive direct and indirect benefits worth up to $1bn from this deal. Denel Aviation, for example, will produce parts for the *Gripen* and *Hawk* jets; in conjunction, Saab and the UK's BAE Systems are providing the company with computer-assisted design (CAD) technology to support these manufacturing operations. Denel will also produce engines and airframes for the A-109 helicopters, as well as performing final assembly on this system. Kentron, meanwhile, would arm South Africa's new corvettes with its *Umkhonto* air-defence system. Other South African firms will produce electro-optical surveillance turrets, avionics suites, electronic-warfare systems, radar and gun systems that will go into a number of imported weapons platforms. In addition, the Europeans have agreed to collaborate with South African arms firms on future third-party exports and to help market South African defence products. Denel will supply components for *Gripen* fighters exported to other countries, while it is also working with Italy to co-produce A-109 helicopters for the Swedish Army.[37]

Just as critical, South Africa has begun to open up its arms industry to foreign strategic equity investment. BAE Systems, for example, has acquired a 51% stake in Paradigm System Technologies (a small South African defence company), as well as 20% of ATE, a local defence electronics firm. Other foreign investment includes the takeover of Reunert's armoured-vehicle subsidiary by the UK's Vickers Defence Systems, the purchase of Reunert's radar and defence-logistics businesses by the European Aeronautic, Defence and Space Corporation (EADS), the acquisition of Altech Defence Systems (renamed African Defence Systems) by Thales of France, and Saab's purchase of a 49% share in Grintek's Avitronics division. In addition, South African arms firms have established a number of joint ventures and strategic alliances with foreign companies. Saab, for example, has formed a joint venture with Grintek to produce electronic-warfare equipment.[38]

The current government views foreign investment in Denel as critical to the company's future. According to the Minister of Public Enterprises, 'strategic equity partners will provide much needed capital injection in the various Denel business units, and greater access to technology and access to markets'.[39] BAE Systems plans to acquire a 20%–30% stake in Denel's Aviation and Ordnance groups once the company is privatised, while Turbomeca is purchasing a majority share in Denel's Airmotive Division.

Overall, South Africa's arms industry is dramatically recasting itself, both structurally and strategically. The defence industry views cooperation and link-ups with first-tier arms-producing states as critical to its survival. In particular, it sees its future in playing an important if niche role as a supplier and systems integrator of sub-systems and components to foreign weapon systems. In this regard, South Africa's arms industry increasingly emphasises its traditional strengths in upgrading and customising foreign weaponry as making it a 'natural partner' in future international collaborative programmes.[40]

Whether this strategy will succeed remains uncertain. It is questionable whether the South African defence industry can find sufficient – particularly foreign – outlets for its few remaining indigenous products. Denel, for example, has nearly given up on securing additional orders for the *Rooivalk* helicopter, while its stand-off weapons and air-to-air missiles must compete in markets already dominated by first-tier suppliers. Furthermore, there are no assurances that many current collaborative activities with foreign defence firms will continue after their offset obligations are met. South African companies must solidify their relationships with the first-tier producers and establish lasting partnerships.

## South Korea: trying to grow out of its problems

Despite the fallout from the 1997–98 financial crisis in Asia, South Korea remains committed to 'acquiring the ability to independently develop primary weapon systems for core force capability'.[41] If anything, the country's economic difficulties have spurred Seoul to put even greater emphasis on 'domestic weapons first' in order to protect foreign-currency reserves, save jobs and aid local industry.[42] Plans for several indigenous weapon systems have been postponed but not abandoned; South Korea still intends to develop an advanced fighter jet by 2015, for example, as well as an indigenous destroyer and several new missile systems.[43] One consequence of this expanded support for the domestic arms industry has been a notable increase in military spending. The overall defence budget grew by 5% in 2000, after remaining static in 1998 and 1999, to reach 5.34 trillion won ($4.3bn), and expenditures on equipment have remained largely shielded from cuts. The military's R&D budget was a record $640m in 1999, or 5.3% of total defence expenditure, and the military intends to increase R&D spending to 10% of its budget by 2015.[44]

At the same time, the 1997–98 crisis spurred Seoul to confront serious over-capacities in its domestic arms industry, as part of its broader campaign to reform and reign in the bloated and over-extended *chaebols* (industrial conglomerates). In 1998, for example, the military initiated a series of studies into rationalising parts of the defence industrial base, including small arms and munitions, armoured vehicles and submarine production. It concluded that approximately half of the work in these sectors should be opened up to competition, in an effort to encourage consolidation.[45]

The most significant outcome of this rationalisation process was the formation in late 1999 of Korea Aerospace Industries (KAI), the result of a merger of three of the country's aircraft companies – Samsung Aerospace, Daewoo Heavy Industries Aerospace Division and Hyundai Space and Aircraft Company. KAI has 3,600 employees and combined annual sales of around $700m, and it controls most of the country's key aerospace manufacturing programmes, including the T-50 advanced trainer/light attack jet, the KT-1 turboprop trainer, the F-16 licenced-production line, UAVs and satellites.[46] In addition, the company performs subcontracting work for foreign aerospace companies, in particular supplying the wings for the Boeing-717 commercial jet.[47] The government has thrown its support behind KAI, pledging that the company will be given exclusive rights to future military aircraft contracts, such as the FX fighter programme and the AHX attack helicopter, as well as promising to fund half of the cost of new commercial aerospace projects.[48]

KAI is the embodiment of many big dreams. It intends to treble its revenues by 2008 and be among the world's top ten aerospace companies by 2010.[49] KAI has especially high hopes for the T-50 jet, which it sees as propelling the company into the leading ranks of the global aerospace industry. The company expects to export 600 to 800 of these aircraft over the next 20 years, at a cost of up to $22m apiece.[50] At the same time, the South Korean government sees KAI – and the aerospace industry in general – as an important symbol of the country's 'coming of age' as a high-technology powerhouse and as a regional power.[51]

South Korea's arms industry has also seen some consolidation of its production capacity. KAI plans to close at least one of its factories, while some smaller defence firms have been permitted to go bankrupt. In 2001, the ordnance manufacturer Hanwha acquired Daewoo's defence-electronics business.[52] South Korea's defence firms have also begun to embrace globalisation in an effort to find new capital, new programmes and greater access to global markets. In late 1999, Samsung Electronics sold a 50% share in its defence-electronics subsidiary to Thales of France. This new joint venture, Samsung Thales, reported sales of $164m in 2000, and has a backlog of orders worth over $300m.[53]

Beyond these few activities, however, South Korea has done little to reform and rationalise its defence industry. In particular, the country's *chaebols* have failed to lay off workers in any significant numbers in this sector. For example, while KAI operates at perhaps

30% of capacity, it plans to eliminate no more than 500 jobs, or less than 15% of its workforce.[54] Moreover, in such areas as munitions (with 12 competing firms), armoured vehicles (three companies) and shipbuilding (five shipyards capable of constructing warships), the government has not forced any firm to exit or consolidate operations.[55] In fact, Seoul was unable to prevent Hyundai's shipbuilding subsidiary from bidding against – and eventually beating – Daewoo's Okpo shipyard for a contract to supply three new submarines to the South Korean Navy, even though Daewoo has long been the country's designated submarine builder.

The creation of KAI solves few of the serious problems plaguing the country's aerospace industry. The company remains saddled with heavy debts. The three aviation firms making up KAI were all operating at a loss prior to the merger, and had debt-to-equity ratios as high as 400%. KAI carries a debt equal to approximately 180% of equity, and it continues to lose money. Small wonder, therefore, that one observer has described the creation of KAI as the 'merger of three dysfunctional firms into one big dysfunctional firm'.[56] KAI does not even consolidate all of the country's aerospace businesses within a single firm. Korean Air – reportedly the country's only profitable aircraft builder – has so far opted out of the new company. In addition, Samsung decided to retain its jet-engine production and overhaul business, rather than fold it into KAI.[57]

KAI must also deal with the long-term challenge of keeping its factories operating. Given delays in the T-50 programme, for example, the company was confronted with the prospect of having to shut down one of its key manufacturing facilities, leaving thousands of workers idle. Consequently, Seoul decided in mid-2000 to build, at a cost of $700m, an additional batch of 20 F-16 fighters – over the objections of South Korea's Air Force, which argued that these aircraft were unwanted and unnecessary – in order to keep KAI in business until T-50 production started up around 2003. Even then, KAI faces another gap in production after 2010, when currently-contracted T-50 production ends.[58]

Commercial aerospace and subcontracting work has provided KAI with little relief. During the 1990s, for example, South Korea's aircraft industry pinned considerable hopes on securing a part in two important international commercial aircraft projects, the 100-seat

AE-100 regional jet and the 70-seat AIR-70 *Twinjet*.[59] Both programmes came to nothing. In addition, after investing nearly $1bn in constructing a new production facility, KAI quietly abandoned wing production for the Boeing-717; due to high overheads and low productivity, the company reportedly lost money on every wing it delivered.[60]

Finally, KAI has failed to secure any foreign investment, which could help to reduce its long-term debt, and bring in new business and new technology. In early 2000, the company considered bids by two international consortiums to acquire a large minority stake in its operations, one consisting of the Boeing Company and BAE Systems, and another comprising Lockheed Martin and France's Aerospatiale Matra. The Lockheed–Aerospatiale group eventually dropped out, and Boeing–BAE began negotiations to acquire a 35% share in KAI for $180m. Talks collapsed, however, when both sides failed to agree on the degree of managerial control that the foreign investors would have in the company. The South Korean government subsequently bailed out KAI with a $440m aid package.[61]

As in other countries, South Korea is trying to expand overseas arms sales as a means of increasing production runs, as well as helping to offset development and production costs. In 1999, South Korean arms exports reached $200m, the highest amount in nearly a decade.[62] Traditionally, however, South Korea has had a tough time breaking into the global arms market, and it has not enjoyed any sustained success as an arms seller; in 2000, for example, arms exports dropped to $55.3m.[63] In addition, South Korean arms exports have consisted mainly of low-tech items such as uniforms, non-lethal military equipment, small arms and ammunition and patrol boats.[64] Although Seoul did win a contract in the mid-1990s to supply Malaysia with 111 KIFV infantry fighting vehicles, and sold seven KT-1 trainer aircraft to Indonesia and self-propelled howitzers to Turkey, such sales have done little to help underwrite advanced arms production.[65] For this, Seoul usually blames its heavy dependence upon US technology, which in turn is subject to US export controls.[66]

One bright spot in the South Korean defence industry is shipbuilding, which has been greatly aided by co-location with commercial production. The national shipbuilding industry is huge – usually first or second largest in the world, in terms of orders – with a multiyear backlog of orders, very efficient and generally profitable.

It annually launches around 100 major commercial vessels, and some shipyards have the capacity to construct up to 25 ships at a time. In contrast, naval shipbuilding barely constitutes one major surface combatant and one submarine a year. Consequently, naval production is well-embedded in – and indirectly subsidised by – a highly productive civilian industry.[67]

Ultimately, South Korea's arms industry expects to grow out of its problems. However, it may be clinging to over-optimistic expectations. KAI, for example, nurtures the ambition of becoming a world-class airframe designer and manufacturer, increasing overall sales by more than 300% (and commercial revenues by over 500%) by 2008.[68] At the same, however, its production capabilities are largely at the low-end of aircraft manufacturing, i.e. bending metal and performing final assembly.[69] Moreover, according to foreign sources in Seoul the company has no real business plan; rather, the hope is that a foreign partner or investor will eventually bring in enough additional work so as to avoid having to take any painful action to deal with over-capacity.[70] South Korea's predictions for arms exports – for example, up to 800 T-50 jets – are equally rosy. Seoul continues to press the US Air Force to purchase the T-50 as a replacement for its T-38 jet trainer, even though the Air Force plans to keep flying its T-38s for the next 20 to 30 years.[71]

## Sweden: globalising for survival

The Swedish authorities have openly acknowledged that autarky in armaments production is no longer 'economically and technically possible',[72] and that the country 'can no longer afford to sustain a national defence industry to the extent that this was possible in the past'.[73] Consequently, Sweden has aggressively pursued a wide range of readjustment strategies, including the consolidation and rationalisation of the national defence industrial base, a concentration on core competencies and niche production and the expanded promotion of arms exports. Above all, Sweden appears to have embraced globalisation more enthusiastically than any other second-tier arms producer, and is currently internationalising much of the process and structure of domestic arms production.

Since the early 1990s, Sweden has been engaged in a dramatic and far-reaching restructuring of its arms industry. In 1991, several of the country's state-owned ordnance, shipbuilding, electronics and aerospace firms were merged to form a new publicly-held entity, Celsius Industries; altogether, Celsius accounted for half of all armaments production in Sweden. Three-quarters of Celsius' stock was openly traded, while the Swedish government kept a 25% 'golden share', equal to 62% of the voting rights. In addition, Saab-Scania AB was broken up in 1995, and its defence and aerospace divisions were hived off into a new separate company called Saab AB. The next big restructuring event occurred in late 1999, when Saab acquired Celsius for $600m. In conjunction with this deal, the government agreed to divest its 25% holding in Celsius, effectively privatising the Swedish defence industry. The new company, renamed Saab Technologies, controls approximately 80% of all Swedish arms production, and boasted 14,000 employees and total annual sales of approximately SEK17bn ($2.2bn) in 2002.[74]

Sweden's arms industry has also undergone significant rationalisation during the 1990s. Defence-related employment has fallen by nearly 50%, from 27,000 workers in 1987 to 14,500 in 1998. Since the end of the Cold War, for instance, Celsius has shrunk by approximately 25%; Bofors alone eliminated 3,500 jobs, nearly 60% of its workforce. Saab, meanwhile, has downsized by nearly 20%, while Volvo Aero declined from 1,900 defence-related jobs in 1993 to 450 by 1998.[75] Defence cuts planned for 2000–2004 could eliminate another 2,000 jobs in the arms industry.[76]

In conjunction with consolidation and rationalisation, core competencies and increased arms exports have become critical facets of Swedish arms production. The new Saab, for example, sees its key competencies as 'information gathering, data fusion, technologies for man-machine interface, decision support, communications, and precision engagement'.[77] Saab regards its major strength as 'systems integration' – 'the ability to assume responsibility for and to implement large-scale projects in which a number of complex systems have to work together'.[78] Consequently, the company intends to focus on a few key sectors, specifically military aircraft, guided weapons, space technology and information technologies for surveillance, command and control. As part of this process, Saab has folded Bofors' missile business into Saab Dynamics, creating a single company offering a complete range of missile systems (air-to-air, air-to-ground, surface-to-air, anti-ship, anti-armour and anti-submarine). At the same time, the company has spun off two of Celsius' former divisions – the Kockums shipbuilding group and Bofors Weapon Systems (ordnance and ammunition) – with the view that they are not in keeping with Saab's new strategic direction.

Saab decided in 1997 to quit the commercial aircraft business, due to flagging sales of its 340 and 2000 commuter planes. The company had ceased production of both aircraft by the end of 1999, although it continues to provide customer support. Saab has at least partly compensated for the loss of these two programmes by expanding *Gripen* production, and increased subcontracting for Airbus Industries. The company builds the main landing gear door for the A340-500/600 airliner, and it is also a risk-sharing partner in the new A3XX super-jumbo project. In 1998, commercial aircraft production accounted for 8% of pre-merger Saab's revenues.[79] Nevertheless, aside from a few such areas of considerable civil–military overlap, Saab intends to concentrate on defence production and to continue to reduce its level of involvement in what it judges to be 'peripheral' operations, such as aircraft leasing, real estate, engineering operations and offshore equipment.[80]

The Swedish defence industry has also placed greater emphasis on diversification and leveraging dual-use technologies for military uses. Saab, for example, increasingly stresses its capabilities as an information technologies company, and its ability to adapt civilian-based IT solutions to military applications.[81] Ericsson Microwave Systems has diversified into the commercial communications sector, such as microwave radio links and base stations, high-speed electronics and network supervision. Much of this was accomplished through military-to-commercial spin-offs, a genuine rarity in post-Cold War defence readjustment. Consequently, the company has moved from being almost entirely defence-dependent to being 60% non-military. Ericsson has used its synergies and technology cross-fertilisation techniques to spin-on commercial solutions for military requirements. Consequently, Ericsson Microwave has developed core competencies in sensors and networking.[82]

The Swedish defence industry has recognised that it can no longer survive solely on domestic orders, and is striving to expand overseas arms sales. Sweden is one of the few second-tier arms producers to have consistently ranked among the world's top ten arms exporters, and during the 1990s it exported around $900m-worth of military equipment annually to around 35–40 countries.[83] Overseas sales account for 25%–30% of the arms industry's output; some companies, such as Saab Training Systems, are almost wholly dependent on arms exports for their revenues.[84]

Swedish defence firms stepped up their promotion of arms exports during the 1990s. Saab – which in the past never seriously pursued fighter exports – has been aggressively marketing the *Gripen* to Central Europe, Latin America and Africa.[85] In late 1999, the company won its first overseas fighter sale in more than 25 years, with an order by South Africa for 28 *Gripens* (nine two-seater aircraft, to be delivered between 2006 and 2009, and 19 single-seaters, for delivery between 2009 and 2011). In 2001, both Hungary and the Czech Republic announced that they would acquire the *Gripen* for their air forces. Despite Prague's later cancellation of its purchase (due to unexpected costs arising from major floods in Summer 2002), the Czechs could still end up buying or leasing *Gripen* fighters; sales to Austria, Brazil and Romania are also possible. Saab projects a potential export market of 200 to 400 *Gripens* over the next 20 years; as such, it is planning on continually upgrading the *Gripen* to keep the aircraft competitive, with new radar, possibly a new engine and thrust vectoring.[86] Other recent Swedish arms exports include submarines to Australia, armoured fighting vehicles to Norway, anti-tank weapons to Austria, Brazil and the US and the *Erieye* airborne early-warning system to Brazil and Greece.

Sweden's arms industry has also enthusiastically embraced the notion that it must globalise in order to survive. According to the country's 1999 defence bill:

> *In order to satisfy the requirement for high-quality materiel, and to facilitate procurement in a situation of internationally increasing armament [costs], greater international collaboration on procurement is called for.*[87]

Sweden was one of six European states to sign a 1998 letter of intent committing these countries to work towards the merger of their aerospace and defence firms and the harmonisation of their arms-export controls. Over the past decade, Swedish defence firms have aggressively pursued numerous collaborative arms activities, including co-development programmes, joint-venture enterprises and even cross-border mergers and acquisitions. In 1995, Saab and British Aerospace (now BAE Systems) agreed to jointly market the *Gripen* fighter to foreign customers; under this arrangement, BAE helped develop an export version of the *Gripen*, and it receives a share of export-related production.[88] The *Gripen* fills a gap in BAE Systems' product line between the *Hawk* advanced trainer jet and the *Eurofighter Typhoon*, while this alliance provides Saab with a worldwide marketing and product-support network. Saab Dynamics is collaborating with EADS on the *Taurus* family of stand-off precision-guided munitions, and with GIAT of France on the *Bonus* 155mm smart artillery projectile. Hägglunds, Sweden's armoured-vehicle manufacturer, is cooperating with Vammos of Finland on the AMOS advanced mortar system. Sweden is also a member of two pan-European consortiums developing the *Meteor* medium-range and IRIS-T short-range AAMs. The Swedish shipbuilder Kockums has a joint venture to build and maintain submarines in Australia, and it has also entered into a consortium with shipyards in Denmark and Norway to co-develop and co-produce a new diesel-powered submarine, codenamed *Viking*. Saab has investments in Norway, Finland, Australia and South Africa. It is also a partner in Nammo, a jointly-owned Swedish–Finnish–Norwegian company producing ammunition. Ericsson Microwave Systems has holdings in Australian, Danish, Norwegian and Polish defence firms, while Hägglunds operates a wholly-owned subsidiary in Norway.

The Swedes have insisted that such international cooperation must be 'combined with measures to safeguard our own competence in strategic areas'.[89] Consequently, arms industries have strongly promoted the concept of arms collaboration and joint venture partnering on the basis of 'earned workshares' – that is, participation based on demonstrated competencies – rather than the more traditional *juste retour* (fair return on investment). Particularly with programmes still in their infancy, such as the *Meteor*, Sweden argues that partnering companies should contribute according to their strengths; as such, Sweden hopes to leverage its technological edge in areas such as sensors, IT and systems integration.[90]

Sweden has also opened up its arms industry to foreign investment and ownership. In 1998, for example, BAE Systems acquired a 35% stake in Saab. This is a significant advance towards the amalgamation of Saab into the rapidly-integrating European defence and aerospace industry. In particular, this alliance strengthens Saab's position in future collaborative arms programmes, and could even pave the way for an eventual merger of Saab into a pan-European defence and aerospace firm. In mid-1999, Celsius merged its Kockums Group with the German submarine builder HDW, to create a new binational shipbuilding company. This new group, in which Saab inherited a 25% share when it acquired Celsius, is a leading supplier of surface and subsurface naval vessels to both the German and Swedish markets. It also dominates the global submarine market and possesses considerable expertise in advanced diesel and air-independent propulsion. In December 2001, Saab sold off its remaining interest in the company to HDW and quit the shipbuilding business altogether. Other acquisitions of Swedish defence firms by foreign companies include the 1997 purchase of Hägglunds by the British firm Alvis and Saab's July 2000 sale of its Bofors Weapon Systems subsidiary to United Defense Ltd., a US builder of self-propelled artillery and armoured vehicles. Consequently, Sweden's naval shipbuilding (both surface combatants and submarines), armoured vehicle and ordnance sectors are all in the hands of foreign owners.

Sweden is in the midst of a major overhaul and reorientation of arms production that, over the next ten to 15 years, promises to radically reshape its defence industry. Overall, Sweden has largely abandoned the aim of self-sufficiency and accepted that much of its future arms procurement and production will be made on the basis of international cooperation. This implies increased foreign dependency, but also increased mutual interdependency and reciprocity. One of the toughest challenges with this tactic is convincing potential foreign partners to accede to this new social contract – in particular, to accept the idea of earned workshares, and that collaboration should be based on core competencies. Moreover, the globalisation of the Swedish arms industry means that the concept of indigenous arms production must also evolve. As one Swedish defence official has put it, 'we do have a defence industry in Sweden, but we don't have anything like a Swedish defence industry'.[91]

## Taiwan: dazed and confused

Officially, Taipei continues to support the concept of a strong domestic arms industry, despite its apparently growing preference for imported weaponry. In 1999, then-President Lee Teng Hui asserted that, while Taiwan may continue to acquire arms from abroad, 'only by enhancing self-development capability can national security be ensured'.[92] This sentiment has been echoed by other officials; the former head of the Chung Shan Institute for Science and Technology (CSIST), for example, has argued that:

> *CSIST is a strategic unit where we have invested a very large*
> *amount of hard currency, and the institute has become one of*
> *our bargaining chips in negotiating with the mainland.*[93]

Nevertheless, given declining prospects for future large defence projects, Taiwan is officially committed to rationalising and converting much of its indigenous arms industry. In the mid-1990s, for example, CSIST announced plans to cut its workforce and greatly curtail its R&D activities; the Aerospace Industry Development Corporation (AIDC) also pledged similar staff reductions.[94] In addition, the government is intent on privatising and commercialising its state-owned aerospace and shipbuilding industries. At one time, it had planned to denationalise AIDC by the end of the 1990s. The company also envisioned selling a sizeable portion of its shares to a 'foreign strategic investor'.[95] In 1996, the government transferred control of AIDC from the Ministry of National Defence to the Ministry of Economic Affairs, and AIDC was subsequently restructured as a state-owned enterprise.[96] Taipei also planned to privatise the China Shipbuilding Corporation (CSC) by late 1997.

Taipei has in particular targeted civilian aerospace as a key business sector ripe for growth and development. AIDC, for example, estimates that, if it remains a mainly military-oriented aerospace company, it will be forced to lay off up to 75% of its workforce.[97] Consequently, since the early 1990s Taipei has encouraged Taiwan's aerospace industry to expand into commercial aviation manufacturing. In 1991, the central government founded the Taiwan Aerospace Corporation (TAC), a joint public–private venture with the central government holding 35% of the company's shares. TAC was supposed to become the centre for Taiwan's commercial aerospace business, and to make Taiwan a major Asian aerospace manufacturer by 2000.[98] In addition, the government detailed plans to establish a special aerospace industrial park (similar to the island's science and technology incubator in Hsinchu) in Taichung, already home to AIDC and several other aircraft companies.[99]

Particular emphasis was placed on Taiwanese companies entering into strategic alliances, joint ventures and subcontracting agreements with foreign aerospace firms. AIDC, for example, has jointly developed and produced the AE-270 small business plane with the Czech firm Aero Vodochody. In addition, the company is collaborating with Sikorsky Aircraft to co-produce the S-92 commercial helicopter, and with Allied Signal on jet engines.[100] AIDC and other Taiwanese aerospace companies are supplying Western manufacturers with parts and components for commercial aircraft. AIDC, for example, is building empennages (tail sections) for the Boeing-717 regional jet, rudders for the Dassault *Falcon*-900 business jet and tail parts for the Alenia C-27 transport aircraft.[101] It is also expanding engine-component production, particularly castings.[102] By becoming a 'reliable' second-tier supplier to Western aerospace firms, AIDC hopes to expand its commercial business to at least 50% of total corporate income by 2010 (compared to 20% in 2000) and treble company revenues to $1bn.[103] The government has also pursued similar plans to revitalise the shipbuilding industry through new commercial projects.[104]

Taiwan, like other countries, is interested in leveraging dual-use commercial technologies for military uses, and the military has at least a declaratory policy of increasing the use of civilian resources. This includes promoting greater cooperation between military R&D organisations such as CSIST and AIDC and local commercial research institutes and industry.[105]

Finally, Taiwan has tried to expand its arms exports. AIDC, in cooperation with Allied Signal, is supplying Aero Vodochody with F124-100 turbofan engines (a derivative of the IDF's TFE-1042 engine) for the Czech Republic's L-159 light combat aircraft programme.[106] In addition, AIDC wants to develop and market internationally a two-seater trainer version of the IDF, as well as upgrading and reselling up to 140 used F-5 fighters being retired from the Air Force.[107]

In reality, however, not much has actually happened to reform and revitalise Taiwan's defence industry. The government has been unwilling or unable to privatise state-owned enterprises;

deadlines to privatise AIDC – first by the end of 1998 and then by the end of 1999 – have come and gone. In late 2000, AIDC announced that it would privatise by the end of 2001 – even then, the government would retain up to 49% of the company – but this goal, too, was missed.[108] In addition, AIDC has resisted efforts to break up the company into several profit-and-loss centres. Consequently, it has been difficult to attract foreign (particularly US) investors.[109] At the CSC, labour opposition and concerns for the company's long-term economic viability have pushed back plans to sell off the shipyard by several years.[110] There are no plans to privatise or commercialise CSIST, which remains directly owned and operated by the Ministry of National Defence.

In addition, Taiwan's state-owned defence enterprises have found it difficult to reduce their workforce significantly. CSIST has reportedly cut around 2,000 jobs since the mid-1990s, but reliable statistics are hard to come by.[111] Other redundancies announced by CSIST turned out to be artificial, attributable mainly to the transfer of AIDC's ownership to the Ministry of Economic Affairs.[112] AIDC has downsized by around 20%, mainly through attrition and early retirement. CSC, meanwhile, laid off around half of its labour force and implemented pay cuts of 35%, and the company returned to profitability in 2002.[113] However, these attempts at workforce rationalisation may not be sufficient to deal with long-term over-capacities and the general lack of work in Taiwan's defence sector.

Attempts to increase Taiwanese arms exports have also been largely unsuccessful, and over the past decade overseas sales have amounted to less than $15m annually (mainly small arms and ammunition).[114] Taiwan faces stiff competition. Sweden, for example, is offering its two-seater *Gripen* as an advanced trainer aircraft, in direct competition with the proposed IDF-based trainer. The US, Belgium and the Netherlands are all trying to sell used F-16s, while several countries are offering services and packages to upgrade older fighters. Taiwanese weapons come with considerable political baggage, and few countries want to risk angering China by buying arms from Taipei.[115]

Finally, Taiwan has made little significant headway in dual-use development and spin-on or defence diversification. Despite CSIST's declared dual-use cooperation and adaptation strategy, successful commercial-to-military spin-on has not materialised. CSC, despite possessing considerable capabilities in design and construction, has struggled in a global commercial shipbuilding sector characterised by low demand and excess capacity.[116] In addition, most of Taiwan's commercial aircraft work remains relatively minor. For all its high expectations, the Taiwan Aerospace Corporation never really took off; consequently, TAC is a minor player in local aviation manufacturing. Taiwan's efforts in the 1990s to buy its way into foreign commercial aircraft programmes mostly ended in failure and disappointment, such as the stillborn McDonnell Douglas MD-12 super-jumbo, a joint venture with British Aerospace to build regional jets. Plans to collaborate with European aerospace firms on a 70-seat regional jet and to participate in the Airbus A380 jumbo jet both collapsed, due to a lack of funding from Taiwan.[117] The AIDC/Aero Vodochody AE-270 business plane programme is badly delayed.[118] In fact, since the conclusion of IDF production in early 2000, AIDC has been without a major aircraft-manufacturing programme.

Taiwan's arms industry appears to have few alternatives but to beg for further government support. The central government is planning to establish a $625m fund to help AIDC invest in foreign aerospace projects.[119] Taipei is increasing defence spending and indigenous arms development as a means of boosting defence-industry employment. The Taiwanese Navy has agreed to acquire an eighth *Perry*-class frigate, along with 30 new 'stealthy' patrol boats, to be built by CSC.[120] AIDC still regards military work as critical to preserving its core engineering and systems-integration capabilities, and in mid-2000 the government initiated a seven-year programme to develop a strike aircraft based on the IDF; this project could be worth as much as $226m to AIDC.[121] CSIST has pressured Taipei to underwrite several new domestic missile and other military programmes, mainly as a means of preserving jobs, and is reportedly transferring some missile-component production to AIDC, in an effort to increase work at the latter's under-utilised aviation facilities.[122]

These measures are, however, only a short-term solution to the challenges facing Taiwan's defence industry. Eventually, both government and industry must deal with the myriad problems of over-capacity, inefficient production and declining demand. Throwing more money at the arms industry will only delay an eventual reckoning.

# Chapter 3

## Towards a Brave New Arms Industry?

Second-tier arms-producing states around the world face a challenging – and in some cases a grim – future. The growing economic and technological demands of advanced arms manufacturing make it unlikely that the second tier of defence industries will expand much over the next ten to 15 years, either quantitatively or qualitatively. Particularly for developing countries, deficiencies at nearly all levels – the national science and technology infrastructure, R&D and advanced manufacturing and production – remain high barriers to developing, absorbing and exploiting advanced technologies for military uses. At the same time, cost-inefficiencies in armaments production – over-capacity and small, delayed and drawn-out production runs – are increasing for nearly all second-tier producers. The growing resource requirements of acquiring sufficient technological capabilities to move forward in armaments production almost guarantee the continued plateauing – or even the regression – of these countries' defence industrial bases on the ladder of production.

### Patterns of Readjustment

Based on the case studies presented here, as well as the experiences of other second-tier arms-producing countries, a pattern of readjustment has become clear. First, most second-tier states have to at least some degree left the defence business. Argentina, Israel, South Africa and Taiwan have either abandoned or are in the process of quitting local fighter-aircraft production. Brazil has given up its armoured-vehicle business, Indonesia is retrenching its aviation industry and Sweden no longer produces tanks or submarines on its own.

At the same time, few second-tier arms producers are likely to abandon armaments production altogether. Despite growing technological hurdles, delays and cost overruns, other factors – particularly perceived national-security imperatives, sunk investment costs and national pride – continue to act strongly on most second-tier arms-producing states. India, for example, remains committed to its Light Combat Aircraft programme, despite it being at least seven years behind schedule, as well as to its *Arjun* tank, which is still not operational after more than a quarter of a century of development.[1]

Nevertheless, most second-tier arms producers understand that they must deal directly and purposefully with the problems of excess manufacturing capacity, preserving defence jobs and finding new sources of revenue. Thus, many have pursued arms exports as a crucial readjustment strategy, with varying degrees of success. It has been especially difficult for small, newcomer arms producers to break into an already-saturated global market dominated by the first-tier producing states, which are often much more market-aware and can frequently offer superior items at lower prices or with innovative purchase arrangements, such as offsets. Of all second-tier states, only Sweden and Israel have met with much success in exporting arms (see Table 2 opposite).

Diversification and defence conversion have likewise met with mixed success. Over the past decade, several second-tier producers – particularly Brazil, China, Israel, South Korea, Sweden and Taiwan – have scored some noteworthy successes in partly converting their defence industries to commercial production. Brazil's Embraer, for example, has emerged as a world-class producer of regional jets, China's missile industry has successfully branched out into the commercial space-launch business and both Chinese and Taiwanese shipbuilders have greatly expanded the civilian side of their operations. In addition, aerospace firms in China, Singapore, South Korea, Sweden and Taiwan have increased their commercial subcontracting, manufacturing components for companies such as Airbus, Boeing, Sikorsky Helicopters and Pratt & Whitney. Nevertheless, diversification has been much more challenging than expected, and in general defence conversion remains risky, with a

**Table 2** Arms exports for selected second-tier arms-producing countries (constant 1997 US$)

| Year | Argentina | Brazil | India | Israel | Japan | Singapore | South Africa | South Korea | Sweden | Taiwan |
|------|-----------|--------|-------|--------|-------|-----------|--------------|-------------|--------|--------|
| 1987 | 91 | 849 | 7 | 1,045 | 157 | 52 | 26 | 65 | 980 | 13 |
| 1988 | 88 | 885 | 0 | 853 | 468 | 63 | 164 | 76 | 1,011 | 25 |
| 1989 | 73 | 134 | 0 | 1,460 | 219 | 110 | 243 | 49 | 913 | 12 |
| 1990 | 23 | 70 | 12 | 820 | 82 | 35 | 59 | 164 | 849 | 12 |
| 1991 | 6 | 91 | 6 | 850 | 11 | 57 | 11 | 68 | 736 | 6 |
| 1992 | 6 | 200 | 0 | 693 | 11 | 33 | 100 | 44 | 942 | 11 |
| 1993 | 151 | 119 | 11 | 675 | 11 | 22 | 205 | 54 | 918 | 11 |
| 1994 | 32 | 190 | 11 | 846 | 11 | 21 | 243 | 42 | 899 | 21 |
| 1995 | 72 | 21 | 5 | 906 | 21 | 31 | 166 | 52 | 1,010 | 10 |
| 1996 | 5 | 0 | 5 | 763 | 20 | 41 | 356 | 31 | 1,220 | 20 |
| 1997 | 0 | 30 | 90 | 370 | 20 | 90 | 370 | 30 | 900 | 20 |

*Source:* US Department of State, *World Military Expenditures and Arms Transfers 1998* (Washington DC: Government Printing Office, 1999)

| China | 1993 | 1994 | 1995 | 1996 | 1997 | 1998 | 1999 | 2000 |
|-------|------|------|------|------|------|------|------|------|
| (in 2000 dollars) | 1,302 | 695 | 794 | 666 | 1,087 | 531 | 312 | 500 |

*Source:* Richard F. Grimmett, *Conventional Arms Transfers to the Developing World, 1993–2000* (Washington DC: Congressional Research Service, 2001)

high potential for failure.[2] Indonesia, Israel, South Korea and Taiwan have all found it difficult to break into civil-aviation manufacturing at the level of a systems integrator or as a major partner in collaborative aircraft programmes. Saab has suffered a particularly severe setback in building commercial aircraft, Brazil's space-launch business has so far been a dud and, while China has converted much of its military-industrial complex to commercial production (at least in terms of output), many of its arms factories are still losing money.

Finally, while the idea of leveraging dual-use technologies has received considerable attention, there has been little actual implementation.[3] Despite the promise of the IT-based revolution in military affairs and the potential impact of dual-use technologies in achieving it, it remains uncertain whether many second-tier arms producers will be able to exploit this avenue of emerging military capabilities. While second-tier countries such as Israel, Japan and Sweden possess strong IT infrastructures, indigenous R&D capabilities are patchy, and many still rely heavily on imported technology.

With very few exceptions such as Sweden, linkages between dual-use IT sectors and defence industries in most second-tier countries remain weak, limiting commercial-to-military spin-on. Overall, it is unclear how these countries see their local IT industries fitting into their military-industrial complexes, or whether their systems-integration skills are sufficient to adapt commercial technologies to military uses. Particularly in China, South Korea, Taiwan and even Japan, the indigenous defence-industrial base is still heavily oriented towards 'bending metal'; the emphasis is still on building 'prestige' platforms, such as aircraft, submarines and tanks, rather than developing military-technical capabilities in areas such as information processing, command and control and communications.[4] Although the dual-use/spin-on option has considerable promise, the approach is novel and it is too early to tell whether it will constitute a successful second-tier readjustment strategy.

Given the limitations of these strategies, second-tier arms-producing states have been forced to pursue more draconian measures. In particular, many have drastically rationalised their operations through privatisation, layoffs and mergers and acquisitions. State-owned defence enterprises in Australia (ADI), Brazil (Embraer), South Africa (Denel), Sweden (Celsius) and Taiwan (AIDC) have either already been or are scheduled to be privatised.

At the same time, Brazil, Israel, South Africa and Sweden have eliminated approximately half of their defence industry workforce (see Table 3 below). Many countries anticipate additional job losses in their arms industries – at least 2,000 in Sweden, 3,500 in Indonesia and 500 in South Korea's aerospace industry.[5] At the same time, consolidation has meant that armaments production in many of these countries is increasingly concentrated within fewer, larger firms.

**Table 3** Workforce reductions in selected second-tier arms-producing countries

| | Defence industry employment (direct and indirect) | Reductions |
|---|---|---|
| **Brazil** (est.) | | |
| 1989 | 40,000 | |
| 1998 | 20,000 | 20,000 |
| **Indonesia** (direct aerospace only) | | |
| 1992 | 15,500 | |
| 2000 | 10,500 | 5,000 |
| **Israel** (state-owned enterprises only) | | |
| 1985 | 43,700 | |
| 1997 | 23,000 | 20,700 |
| **South Africa** | | |
| 1990 | 130,000 | |
| 1997 | 50,000 | 80,000 |
| **Sweden** (direct only) | | |
| 1987 | 27,000 | |
| 1998 | 14,500 | 12,500 |
| **Taiwan** (est., direct only) | | |
| 1990 | 23,700 | |
| 2000 | 20,700 | 3,000 |

*Sources*: Bonn International Center for Conversion; 'Taiwan's Troubles', *Flight International*, 7 August 2001; Swedish Defense Industry Association; *White Paper on the South African Defense-Related Industries*; 'New Flight Plan', *Far Eastern Economic Review*, 2 March 2000.

In conjunction, many second-tier states – particularly Brazil, Israel, Singapore, South Africa and Sweden – appear to have adopted a core competencies/niche production approach. Israel has carved out particular strengths in UAVs, air-to-air missiles, reconnaissance and surveillance systems and electro-optics, while Singapore has developed a strong niche in aircraft-upgrade packages. South Africa's arms industry emphasises its strengths in ruggedised communications systems, long-range artillery and UAVs, as well as its ability to modify and update equipment for unique environments. Sweden's Saab is increasingly focused on military aircraft, guided weapons, space and C4ISR (command, control, communications, computing, intelligence, surveillance and reconnaissance) technologies.

Finally, the second-tier arms-producing states appear to be increasingly swept up in the same globalisation process that is transforming the rest of the world's defence industries. The escalating resource demands of state-of-the-art arms production are driving both first- and second-tier producers to internationalise their operations, in order to leverage technology breakthroughs, rationalise military R&D and production, increase efficiencies and economies of scale and penetrate foreign markets. Since the end of the Cold War, therefore, the major defence firms in the US and Western Europe have greatly expanded their transnational operations, with teaming arrangements, strategic alliances, joint-venture companies and even mergers and acquisitions. This globalisation process has been mainly industry-led; industry, rather than the state, has taken the initiative in crafting an international defence industry.[6]

In fact, globalisation has increasingly become the norm among the first-tier arms-producing states, particularly in Western Europe.[7] Britain's BAE Systems, for example, is as large a player in the US arms market as it is in the UK or in Europe more widely. France's Thales is home-based in ten countries. Nearly all European armaments production is now collaborative, and increasingly rooted in transnational enterprises such as Eurocopter (a Franco-German helicopter joint venture), MBDA (an Anglo-French-Italian missile company) and Astrium (a British-French-German-Italian satellite builder). Defence-industry globalisation in Western Europe reached a climax in late 1999, with the merger of DASA of Germany, France's Aerospatiale Matra and CASA of Spain into the new European Aeronautic, Defense and Space Corporation (EADS).

Only in the last few years has this globalisation process begun to include the second-tier states. Nevertheless, this phenomenon appears to be accelerating, especially as second-tier producers increasingly see few viable autarkic alternatives. In fact, nearly every second-tier producer either already has, or else is attempting to secure, some type of foreign strategic equity shareholding regarding some component of their domestic arms industry (see Table 4 over). Many defence firms in second-tier countries are increasingly pursuing international joint ventures and teaming arrangements.

Overall, many second-tier producers rely heavily on globalisation as a survival strategy. South Africa's arms industry sees its future in playing an important if niche role as a supplier and systems integrator of subsystems and components to foreign weapon systems.[8] South Korea's KAI is teamed with Lockheed Martin on the T-50 jet fighter, while Brazil's Embraer-170/-190 family of regional jets will be built in a risk-sharing partnership with over a dozen companies around the world. Sweden has implicitly abandoned the idea of an autarkic arms industry, and thrown open its defence sector to the global marketplace.

## The emerging 'hub-and-spoke' of global arms production

The readjustment efforts of second-tier arms producers appear to underscore the necessity of some measure of defence-industry rationalisation and globalisation. As this process develops, it could have a significant impact on the basic structure and nature of arms production worldwide. In general, the global arms industry over the next ten to 15 years is likely to become:

- *smaller*, as worldwide armaments production continues to decline and manufacturing capacity contracts, and as most second- and even some first-tier states abandon certain types of indigenous arms production;

- *more concentrated*, as armaments production is consolidated in the hands of fewer and bigger companies and countries (both in the first- and second-tier arms-producing states); and

- *more integrated*, as the globalisation process gains momentum and as more armaments production is carried out transnationally – dominated and controlled by first-tier states.

**Table 4** Globalisation activities in selected second-tier arms-producing countries

**I. Foreign direct investment in second-tier defence firms**

| Country | Acquired firm | Acquiring first-tier firm | Products |
|---|---|---|---|
| Argentina | FMA (100%) | Lockheed Martin (US) | Aircraft maintenance and upgrades |
| Australia | Siemens Plessy Electronics Australia (100%) | BAE Systems (UK) | Electronics |
| Australia | Land Rover Australia (100%) | BAE Systems (UK) | Military vehicles |
| Australia | AeroSpace Technologies of Australia (ASTA) (100%) | Boeing (US) | Aircraft components |
| Australia | Hawker deHavilland of Australia (100%) | Boeing (US) | Aircraft components |
| Australia | Australian Aerospace (100%) | EADS (France, Germany, Spain) | Aircraft repair |
| Australia | Australian Defence Industries (50%) | Thales (France) | Naval vessels, armoured vehicles, artillery |
| Australia | Wormald Technology (100%) | Thales (France) | Simulators |
| Brazil | Embraer (20%) | Dassault, EADS, Snecma, Thales (France) | Aircraft |
| Canada | Canadian Marconi (100%) | BAE Systems (UK) | Electronics |
| Canada | Oerliken Aerospace (100%) | Rheinmetall (Germany) | Missiles |
| Czech Republic | Aero Vodochody (35%) | Boeing (US) | Fighter aircraft |

| Country | Company | Partner | Products |
|---|---|---|---|
| Israel | Galaxy Aerospace (100%) | General Dynamics (US) | Regional jets |
| Singapore | Avimo (17%) | Alvis (UK) | Electro-optical systems |
| Singapore | Avimo (42%) | Thales (France) | Electro-optical systems |
| South Africa | Denel (20%) (planned) | BAE Systems (UK) | Aircraft, missiles, electronics |
| South Africa | Paradigm Systems (100%) | BAE Systems (UK) | Aircraft engineering |
| South Africa | ATE (20%) | BAE Systems (UK) | UAVs, avionics |
| South Africa | Reutech Radar Systems (100%) | EADS (France, Germany, Spain) | Radar, electronics |
| South Africa | Denel Swartklip (100%) | Pains Wessex (UK) | Pyrotechnics |
| South Africa | Altech Defence Systems (100%) | Thales (France) | Systems integration |
| South Africa | Denel Airmotive (100%) | Turbomeca (France) | Aeroengines |
| South Africa | Reumech OMC (100%) | Vickers (UK) | Armoured vehicles |
| South Korea | Samsung Electronics (50%) | Thales (France) | Electronics |
| Spain | Santa Barbara | General Dynamics (US) | Tanks, Armoured vehicles |
| Sweden | Saab (35%) | BAE Systems (UK) | Aircraft, missiles, electronics |
| Sweden | Bofors Weapon Systems (100%) | United Defense (US) | Artillery and ordnance |
| Sweden | Hagglunds (100%) | Alvis (UK) | Armoured vehicles |
| Sweden | Kockums (100%) | HDW (Germany) | Submarines, surface combatants |
| Switzerland | MOWAG (100%) | General Motors Canada (US/Canada) | Armoured vehicles |

**Table 4** Globalisation activities in selected second-tier arms-producing countries *continued*

**II. International joint ventures involving second-tier arms-producing countries**

| Country | Company | First-tier company | Products |
|---|---|---|---|
| Brazil | Helibras | Aerospatiale Matra (France) | Helicopters |
| Brazil | Imbel | BAE Systems (UK) | Ordnance |
| Israel | Israeli Military Industries | Primex (US) | Ordnance |
| Malaysia | Sapura | Thales (France) | Communications equipment |
| Singapore | ST Aerospace | BAE Systems (UK) | Aircraft parts |
| Singapore | ST Aerospace | Messier-Dowty (France) | Landing gear |
| Singapore | ST Aerospace, SBE | BAE Systems (UK) | Military/civil training facility |
| Singapore | ST Chartered Industries | Thales (France) | Electronics |
| South Africa | Grintek Comms | EADS (France, Germany, Spain) | Communications equipment |
| South Africa, Sweden | Grintek, Saab | n/a | 'Grintek Avitronics' (avionics) |
| Sweden, Norway, Finland | Bofors, Kongsberg, Patria | n/a | 'Nammo' (ordnance) |
| Turkey | Nurol | United Defense (US) | 'FNSS' (armoured vehicles) |
| Turkey | TAI | Lockheed Martin (US) | 'TUSAS' (F-16 co-production) |

III. International teaming involving second-tier arms-producing countries

| Country | Company | First-tier company | Products |
|---------|---------|-------------------|----------|
| Brazil | Embraer | Alenia, Aeromacchi (Italy) | AMX fighter jet |
| Canada | Bombardier | SAT (France) | CL-289 UAV |
| Chile | FAMAE | BAE Systems (UK) | Ordnance, multiple rocket launcher |
| Indonesia | IPTN | EADS (CASA) | CN-235 transport aircraft |
| Israel | Elbit | Rockwell Collins (US) | Helmet-mounted displays |
| Israel | Israeli Aircraft Industries | AAI Corp. (US) | *Pioneer* UAV |
| Japan | KHI | Eurocopter (France) | BK-117 helicopter |
| Japan | Mitsubishi Heavy Industries | Lockheed Martin (US) | F-2 fighter |
| Singapore | ST Engineering | Vickers (UK) | Armoured vehicles, artillery |
| Singapore, China | ST Aerospace/CATIC | Eurocopter (France) | EC-120 helicopter |
| South Korea | LG | Thales (France) | *Chonma* SAM |
| South Korea | Korea Aerospace Industries | Lockheed Martin (US) | T-50 advanced trainer |

Such a smaller, more consolidated, and more intricately inter-connected global arms industry has many implications for second-tier producers. First, the recent experiences of the second-tier arms-producing states stand as a cautionary tale for other nations attempting to establish their own indigenous arms industries. While the ladder-of-production model may be more or less discredited, many aspiring arms producers – such as Iran and North Korea – continue to cling to it as a means of developing local arms industries. One should expect, however, that these countries will likely encounter many of the same difficulties and setbacks in their efforts as have Brazil, South Africa, and Taiwan. As such, one should not be surprised to see these countries experiencing severe technical problems and programme delays, cost escalations, and, in many cases, less-than-impressive indigenous weapon systems being produced.

Second, there are indicators of an emerging division of labour within the global arms industry, involving both first- and second-tier producer states. The global armaments industry has long been recognised as stratified and hierarchical, according to the technological capabilities and capacities of national defence industries. Increasingly, however, this structure is becoming permanently interconnected and integrated through two-way production linkages, as globalisation involves making second-tier arms industries subsidiaries of, or junior partners to, first-tier companies. Second-tier defence firms are increasingly and formally subordinating themselves to first-tier companies, through subcontracting relationships, joint-venture partnerships and foreign equity ownership. Plans for self-sufficient arms production within the second tier are being supplanted by a return to greater degrees of dependence upon foreign armaments and technologies, either through off-the-shelf imports, licensed production or co-development programmes. This approach is not limited to second-tier producers in the developing world – even Japan has apparently reinterpreted its autarkic defence-industrial strategy to emphasise more bilateral development with the US.[9]

As a result, a truly globalised arms industry could be emerging, akin to the 'core–periphery' concept of international industrial organisation.[10] Structurally, such a system could resemble a huge 'hub and spoke' model: a few large first-tier firms operating at the centre, with lines of outsourced production extending to second-tier states on the periphery. First-tier players would serve as 'centres of excellence', providing armaments production with its critical design, development and systems-integration inputs, along with the production of more advanced subsystems, such as engines, wings, sensors, information systems and other electronics. Second-tier arms-producers would mainly be responsible for supplying niche systems or low-tech items, such as structural components. Final assembly could take place in either country, depending on the end-user. Such cooperative arrangements could be highly formalised, involving a second-tier firm working for only one first-tier producer, presumably as a wholly- or partially-owned subsidiary. It is, however, more likely that this process would entail second-tier enterprises being engaged in subcontracts or joint-venture partnerships with several first-tier firms at the same time. As such, future armaments production could more closely resemble the modern concept of the 'virtual corporation' – independent firms coming together on an as-needed basis in order to design and/or develop and/or manufacture a product, only on a global scale.

Within such a process of globalised armaments production, second-tier states would essentially leverage their main comparative advantages: niche strengths, manpower, money and markets. It is already apparent that many second-tier producers are increasingly using the core-competencies strategy to emphasise the unique contributions they can make to international joint weapon programmes.[11] Many second-tier arms producers – particularly those in the developing and newly-industrialised economies – have a considerable advantage in being able to offer a relatively high-quality, low-cost workforce. Cheap labour has particularly worked to the advantage of countries such as China, South Korea and Taiwan in securing subcontracting work from Western aerospace firms. As the costs of weapon systems escalate, first-tier arms manufacturers may increasingly look to place certain (particularly low-tech) pieces of production 'off-shore', to low-cost second-tier states.

Many second-tier states are also prepared to make considerable investments in international arms programmes in order to secure a possible part in production. Taiwan's government, for example, is establishing a multimillion-dollar fund to help local aerospace firms to invest in foreign projects.[12] Several second-tier countries, including Australia, Canada, Norway and Turkey, have joined the US Joint Strike Fighter programme, while Japan is considering buying its way into US theatre-missile defence. Finally, second-tier countries could exploit their ability to restrict access to domestic arms markets in order to pressure first-tier firms to give them a better deal in subcontracting and offset arrangements.

For the second-tier arms producers, repositioning themselves to play a subordinate role in such a globalised division of labour may make considerable economic and technological sense. It is perhaps the most cost-effective way to preserve and maintain national defence industries – and especially the jobs within them. It also permits many second-tier arms industries to make maximum use of their few competitive advantages in the global arms market, while keeping these industries open to cross-fertilisation from foreign technologies; indeed, one of the greatest drawbacks to autarky is the risk of inadvertently isolating one's defence industrial base from innovative foreign technologies, foreign capital and global markets.

Obviously, such subordination represents a major departure from the concept of self-sufficiency which has long been the second-tier countries' primary aim in establishing indigenous defence industries in the first place. Even if self-sustaining autarky was ultimately an illusion – and an unaffordable one, at that – consciously abandoning this goal is still a difficult and even traumatic move for many second-tier producers. It demands that these countries increasingly concede a formal, pervasive and perhaps even irreversible dependence on foreign defence industries and technologies, and accept the fact that they will be more vulnerable to foreign political-economic manipulation – particularly through threats of embargoes or sanctions. Furthermore, globalisation entails a fundamental shift away from protecting and nurturing an insular indigenous defence industrial base, and towards exposing these firms to the often-harsh economic realities of the global arms marketplace.

Consequently, many second-tier producer-states will probably try to preserve at least some capacity for autarkic arms production. Some countries, such as South Korea or Japan, have in fact consciously used international armaments collaboration as a means of extracting technical-industrial concessions (such as technology transfers or production offsets) in support of indigenous arms industries. In addition, while most second-tier states may abandon autarky in such areas as combat aircraft, tactical missile systems, main battle tanks, warships and submarines, they are likely to remain heavily engaged in indigenous defence manufacturing at either end of the technological extreme: small arms and munitions, and weapons of mass destruction (WMD).

With regard to the former, the technologies surrounding the development and manufacture of items such as assault rifles, artillery, mortars, mines and ammunition are relatively mature, well-diffused and easier to absorb. Moreover, there generally exists a constant domestic market for these products, providing a reliable core customer, while the export market also tends to be more open, less dominated by a few big countries and often quite lucrative. At the other end of the spectrum, a second-tier producer might choose to invest in developing a nuclear, chemical or biological weapons capability and a companion missile delivery system. India, Iran, North Korea and Pakistan all show indications of preferring a 'WMD solution' as at least a partial means of overcoming the deficiencies in their conventional arms industries. In addition, states such as South Korea and Taiwan might also increasingly choose to emphasise WMD development and production; both countries, in fact, are already considering boosting indigenous ballistic-missile development.

Some second-tier countries will always remain committed to preserving a high degree of autarky, and will be prepared to pay the price. This is certainly evident in the case of China. Despite persistent technological setbacks and economic problems afflicting its military-industrial complex, Beijing continues to stress self-sufficiency in arms production as a strategic necessity. Consequently, readjustment has been directed towards conserving the Chinese arms industry, and has generally avoided tough decisions over which sectors to nurture and which to reduce, abandon or subordinate to foreign interests. Despite considerable over-capacity, over-manning and redundancy – resulting in inefficient production, huge economic losses and heavy debts – Beijing has largely resisted rationalising and 'marketising' China's defence industry, or opening up indigenous production to the globalisation process. The breakup of old state-owned enterprises such as Aviation Industries of China (AVIC) or the North China Industrial Group (Norinco) into new 'industrial enterprise groups' has generally failed to inject greater competition and market-oriented thinking into China's military-industrial complex. In fact, with few exceptions, these new groups do not compete directly with each other.[13] Rationalisation of the workforce has also been much slower and much less radical than once envisioned. AVIC, for example, was expected to lay off up to a third of its labour force between 1998 and 2000; in reality, only a handful of workers were let go.[14] Finally, when it comes to globalisation China's international collaborative arms activities have mainly been *tactical* – that is, focused on the acquisition of enabling technologies, such as designs, critical subsystems, machine tools and 'know-how' to support indigenous production.[15]

For its part, South Korea still clings to the goal of eventually becoming a major arms producer. KAI, for example, plans to be among the world's top ten aerospace companies by 2010.

Some second-tier states – China, Russia and perhaps even India or Israel – are likely to opt out of the Western-dominated hub-and-spoke model and attempt to retain considerable indigenous and panoramic arms-manufacturing capabilities. Some of these countries may even serve as significant sources of defence systems and technologies to other second-tier producers, competing as alternative hubs with the first-tier states. Russia is already a major supplier of licensed-produced weaponry, defence technology and production know-how, as well as critical subsystems to the Chinese, Indian and Iranian military-industrial complexes. China, meanwhile, has exported some of its home-grown defence technologies (particularly missile systems) to countries such as Pakistan and Iran. India apparently refuses to abandon its dream of a largely self-sufficient defence industry and, despite enduring technological problems and setbacks, still greatly limits foreign participation in indigenous arms production.[16] For its part, Israel constitutes a 'mini-hub' of its own, offering its services as a designer and systems integrator on such items as command-and-control and surveillance systems and stand-off precision-guided attack munitions.

The dilemma for these 'outlier' countries is whether they can continue to afford such a strategy and, even then, whether the results will be worthwhile technologically. Experience has demonstrated that such autarkic and introverted second-tier arms industries will almost invariably continue to lag far behind the first-tier industrialised states in technological innovation and implementation. As Raymond Vernon and Ethan Kapstein noted more than a decade ago:

> *Any nation that is determined to rely upon its own products,*
> *its own technologies, and its own enterprises to fulfill its*
> *defense needs will pay a far higher premium for such a policy*
> *than in years past, costs that will be expressed not only in*
> *terms of money but also in a sacrifice in the quality of its*
> *military equipment.*[17]

In fact, most of these outlier states possess only isolated pockets of excellence upon which they can trade, and many of these are increasingly facing competition from the more dynamic defence industrial bases in the first tier. In Russia, for example, military R&D has largely come to a standstill, given the country's economic difficulties, and most defence establishments are largely selling off their existing core capabilities; this provides them with little to trade in the future. Increasingly, therefore, the only choices for most second-tier arms producers could be globalisation or marginalisation.

# Conclusion

## Implications and Challenges Ahead

Overall, today's global arms industry may, on a superficial level, appear relatively unchanged from the Cold War past. The total number of second-tier arms-producing states has remained roughly constant, and many of these countries may actually be involved in the production of an increasing array of sophisticated weapon systems. Upon closer inspection, however, the global arms industry is undergoing a dramatic evolution. Second-tier states appear to be more dependent than ever on the first-tier producers for critical technologies, components, capital and jobs. As the arms market has contracted and industry has rationalised operations, the bulk of armaments production has become more of a global, integrated and hierarchical affair. Over the next 10–15 years, this trend will accelerate and deepen, along the lines of the hub-and-spoke model.

The emergence of such an intertwined and hierarchical global arms industry – and one increasingly oriented around an international division of labour – has many implications. Obviously, the globalisation of the arms industry presents many potential challenges for international security, especially arms control. Globalisation – as opposed to highly visible, off-the-shelf arms exports – often entails the spread of the intrinsic capabilities for arms production: weapons technologies and production know-how, along with the relatively low-visibility trade in subsystems and components. Therefore, it often constitutes a nearly-indiscernible form of proliferation to second-tier arms-producers in the developing world.[1] Such collaboration, involving as it does the permanent transfer of resources, skills and technologies that underlie armaments production, is potentially more destabilising than outright arms sales.

A smaller global arms industry does not necessarily mean a more secure world. As many second-tier producers embrace a niche production strategy, the incentive to export is increasing; domestic defence markets are too small to support a highly-specialised product line, and economies of scale can only be achieved through overseas sales. In addition, many first-tier/second-tier collaborative arms projects explicitly anticipate joint production for export to third-party countries.[2] This could greatly complicate efforts to control the proliferation of advanced conventional arms.

Globalisation also has the potential to affect regional political and military balances. Technology is often a crucial determinant of military effectiveness and advantage, and the 'possession of modern weapons is a key element in determining the international hierarchy of power'.[3] Hence, it has been argued that the diffusion of military-related technologies (especially dual-use technologies, which are subject to much less scrutiny) and the creation of new centres of arms production are affecting the distribution of power in international relations.[4] Should countries such as China, India, Iran and North and South Korea continue, with outside assistance, to upgrade their military-industrial complexes – even fitfully and to a limited degree – this could eventually have a profound impact on regional balances of power. It could even undermine Western – particularly US – military-technological advantages.

Finally, as Western defence firms become more transnational, their domestic identities and loyalties could begin to blur, making it more difficult to expect them to regulate their potential proliferation activities. At the same time, government controls to prevent companies from engaging in activities threatening to national interests are weakening, as state-owned firms are privatised and/or as they are increasingly expected to wean themselves off their dependence on domestic arms purchases. A globalised defence industry could translate into 'a few, large transnational contractors facing a wider array of buyers'; as a result, 'market power will shift from governments to the private sector'.[5]

The challenge to Western policymakers, therefore, is how to best promote globalisation's benefits while ensuring that this process does not adversely affect national security. The globalisation of the arms industry is in many ways not only desirable but increasingly unavoidable, as the costs of state-of-the-art military equipment continue to rise faster than most countries' defence budgets, and as industry increasingly takes the initiative in internationalising its operations. Nevertheless, any decision to permit the transfer of military technologies or arms-producing capabilities must carefully balance defence-industrial needs against other security interests or, to put it facetiously, to distinguish between 'good' globalisation and 'bad' globalisation.

In particular, Western controls over the export of militarily useful (including dual-use) technologies need to be re-examined and reoriented in light of the globalisation paradigm. Policymakers need to clearly delineate between what manner of technology transfers and international collaboration they should constrain and what sort they should encourage – in other words, erect higher barriers around fewer technologies. Such a technology-control regime should probably be approached multilaterally, with the US and Europe working together to standardise and equalise export controls. In fact, some progress along these lines was made during the last years of the Clinton administration, culminating with the announcement of the Defense Trade Security Initiative (DTSI) in 2000. However, much work still needs to be done.[6]

Given that the inadvertent leakage of some technology is inevitable, policymakers should determine where stricter controls might be ineffective or even counter-productive. This is almost certainly the case with globalisation activities involving the transfer of commercial dual-use technologies, such as information technologies, telecommunications and microelectronics, where restrictive export regulations could severely constrain international trade, to the detriment of supplier and buyer alike. Perhaps the best way for supplier states to guard against the negative repercussions of such activities is to ensure that they maintain their military-technological edge over potential competitors. Such an effort would, in turn, entail a strong political and financial commitment to preserving and enhancing national defence technology and industrial bases.

At the same time, defence-industry globalisation and the emerging hub-and-spoke model of international arms production actually offer innovative solutions for restricting the activities of second-tier arms industries and countering the proliferation behaviour of many developing countries. First, while the globalisation process has certainly caused more sophisticated bits and pieces of arms production to spread to many developing and newly-industrialised countries, it has also meant that these countries' defence industries are increasingly controlled by first-tier defence firms. For many second-tier states, first-tier cooperation and foreign investment have often resulted in decidedly junior partnerships and the abandonment of autarky in exchange for jobs and the promise of workshares. In addition, globalisation and increasing second-tier dependencies could result in new 'technology chokepoints', providing supplier states with opportunities to block the efforts and capabilities of many second-tier producer-states to develop and produce their own weapon systems. Paradoxically, therefore, defence-industry globalisation, rather than diffusing power out to states on the periphery, could actually strengthen Western checks over many arms producers in the developing world, and help to reinforce the current global balance of power.

Second, as second-tier states reduce or even abandon indigenous military R&D in favour of relying on first-tier states for critical technologies, subsystems and system-integration capabilities, their capacity to engage in independent, self-sustaining armaments production could atrophy. Consequently, fears that globalisation could lead to the emergence of 'new centres of production and proliferation' may be greatly mitigated.[7]

Third, in keeping with liberal theories of international cooperation, a growing interdependency in arms production may in itself make a positive contribution to international security. The international division of labour in arms production means that both first- and second-tier states are beholden to each other for critical military systems and subsystems. In particular, first-tier states are increasingly finding themselves more dependent upon defence subcontractors and vendors beyond their borders. As such, the arms industry could become more like other forms of international trade and business, creating another mechanism for cooperation.

Finally, it is premature to assert that globalisation will mean the end of governmental authority over national arms industries and armaments production. While industry is certainly in the driver's seat when it comes to globalisation, the state has not abandoned its right to regulate and ultimately decide how this process will play out. As Keith Hayward argues:

> *As long as international politics remain centered largely, although not exclusively, on the sovereign nation-state, national governments ... are unlikely to disengage entirely from the business of defense production.*[8]

Consequently, governments will remain critical 'gatekeepers, controlling access and determining defense industrial structures'.[9]

An increasingly globalised and hierarchical defence industry promises to radically transform how arms are designed, developed, manufactured and marketed. The emerging hub-and-spoke model has particular implications for the second-tier arms-producing states. However much many of these countries may not like it, for most of them there are few practical alternatives to the further rationalisation and globalisation of their national defence industries. The growing technological and economic demands of advanced conventional arms manufacturing are increasingly impelling these states to this difficult but inevitable conclusion. The biggest challenge for many second-tier countries, therefore, may be accepting this reality and adjusting their arms industries – structurally, operationally and psychologically – to more limited and subordinate circumstances within the global defence-industrial system.

# Notes

## Acknowledgements

The author would like to express his deepest gratitude to the Atlantic Council of the United States and to the Center for the Study of Intelligence for their invaluable support in the researching and writing of this paper. The author also thanks Ian Anthony, Myeong-Chin Cho, Sunjin Choi, Masako Ikegami-Andersson, Martin Lundmark, Ann Markusen, Stephanie Neuman, Erik Pages and Zach Selden for their comments and suggestions on earlier drafts.

The analyses and opinions expressed in this paper are strictly those of the author, and should not be interpreted as representing those of any organisation, institution or agency, public or private.

## Introduction

[1] According to the US State Department, global defence spending fell by nearly 43% between 1987 and 1997. Military expenditures as a percentage of global gross national product (GNP) fell by half, from 5.2% to 2.6%, while worldwide per-capita spending on defence dropped from $271 to $145. The size of the world's armed forces declined from 28.7 million personnel in 1987 to 22.3m in 1997, and the value of the global arms trade fell from $80 billion in 1987 to around $43bn in the mid-1990s. Department of State, Bureau of Verification and Compliance, *World Military Expenditures and Arms Transfers 1998* (Washington DC: US Government Printing Office (USGPO), 2000), pp. 1–2, 6, 19. Admittedly, the US has reversed a 15-year decline in military expenditures, adding more than $20bn to its defence budget in FY2002 and $48bn in FY2003. China continues to pump additional funds into its defence budget, and Beijing effectively doubled military expenditures in real terms between 1989 and 2000. However, few other arms-

producing countries seem prepared to match the US or China in significantly boosting their defence budgets.

2  See Stephanie G. Neuman, 'Industrial Stratification and Third World Military Industries', *International Organization*, Winter 1984, pp. 191–97.

3  Keith Krause, for example, defines the first tier of arms suppliers as the 'critical innovators' at the technological frontier of arms production, and confines this group to the US and the former Soviet Union. He places most of Western Europe into a second tier of 'adapters and modifiers' of advanced military technologies. Finally, all remaining arms-producing countries he puts into a third tier of 'copiers' and 'reproducers' of existing defence technologies. See Keith Krause, *Arms and the State: Patterns of Military Production and Trade* (Cambridge: Cambridge University Press, 1992), pp. 26–33. Andrew Ross accepts Krause's definition of the first tier (the US and the former Soviet Union), but places China, along with the major arms producers in the industrialised world (France, Germany, Italy, Japan, Sweden and the UK) into his category of second-tier producers. Ross then classifies as 'third-tier' most other arms-producing countries – the developing, newly industrialised and smaller industrialised nations, such as Brazil, India, Israel, South Korea and Taiwan. He also has a 'fourth tier' of countries with only limited capabilities, for instance Mexico and Nigeria.

Andrew L. Ross, 'Full Circle: Conventional Proliferation, the International Arms Trade and Third World Arms Exports', in Kwang-il Baek, Ronald. D. McLaurin and Chung-in Moon (eds), *The Dilemma of Third World Defense Industries* (Boulder, CO: Westview Press, 1989), pp. 1–31.

4  Elisabeth Sköns and Reinhilde Weidacher, 'Arms Production', in *SIPRI Yearbook 1999* (Oxford: Oxford University Press for the Stockholm International Peace Research Institute (SIPRI), 1999), pp. 405–11.

5  Barry Buzan, 'The Diffusion of Military Technology: Looking Backward, Looking Forward?', paper delivered to the IISS/NIC conference on 'Transformation in Global Defence Markets and Industries', London, 4–5 November 2000, p. 11.

**Chapter 1**

1  Carol Evans, 'Reappraising Third-World Arms Production', *Survival*, March–April 1986, pp. 100–101; Janne E. Nolan, *Military Industry in Taiwan and South Korea* (New York: St Martin's Press, 1986), pp. 12–14; Ralph Sanders, *Arms Industries: New Suppliers and Regional Security* (Washington DC: NDU Press, 1990), pp. 11–17; Michael Brzoska and Thomas Ohlson, 'Conclusions', in Brzoska and Ohlson (eds), *Arms Production in the Third World 1971–1985* (Oxford: Oxford University Press, 1987), pp. 279–80.

2  James P. McWilliams, *Armscor: South Africa's Arms Merchant* (London: Brassey's, 1989), pp. 2, 179–81; Signe Landgren, *Embargo Disimplemented: South Africa's Military Industry*

(Oxford: Oxford University Press, 1989), pp. 63–123.

3  G. M. Steinberg, 'Israel: High-Technology Roulette', in Brzoska and Ohlson (eds), *Arms Production in the Third World 1971–1985*, pp. 163–67; US Congress, Office of Technology Assessment (OTA), *Global Arms Trade: Commerce in Advanced Military Technology and Weapons* (Washington DC: USGPO, 1991), p. 94; Sharon Sadeh, 'The Israeli Defense Industry: The End is Nigh?', paper presented to the IISS/NIC conference on 'Transformation in Global Defense Markets'.

4  Jong Chul Choi, 'South Korea', in Ravinder Pal Singh (ed.), *Arms Procurement Decision Making, Volume I: China, India, Israel, Japan, South Korea and Thailand* (Oxford: Oxford University Press, 1998), p. 185.

5  Masako Ikegami-Andersson, *The Military-Industrial Complex: The Cases of Sweden and Japan* (Aldershot: Dartmouth Press, 1992), p. 70; Tomas Ries, 'Sweden's Defense at the Crossroads', *International Defense Review*, December 1989.

6  Joseph Kruzel, 'New Challenges for Swedish Security Policy', *Survival*, November–December 1988, p. 538.

7  Bates Gill and Taeho Kim, *China's Arms Acquisitions from Abroad: A Quest for 'Superb and Secret Weapons'* (Oxford: Oxford University Press, 1995), pp. 8–47.

8  Michael J. Green, *Arming Japan: Defense Production, Alliance Politics, and the Postwar Search for Security* (New York: Columbia University Press, 1995), pp. 22–26.

9  Susan Willett, 'East Asia's Changing Defence Industry', *Survival*, Autumn 1997, p. 114; Tim Huxley and Susan Willett, *Arming East Asia* (Oxford: Oxford University Press for the IISS, July 1999), p. 51.

10  Jong Chul Choi, 'South Korea', in Ravinder Pal Singh (ed.), *Arms Procurement Decision Making, Volume I*; Patrice Franko-Jones, *The Brazilian Defense Industry* (Boulder, CO: Westview Press, 1992), pp. 55–63; Janne E. Nolan, 'South Korea: Ambitious Client of the United States', in Brzoska and Ohlson (eds), *Arms Production in the Third World 1971–1985*, pp. 218–19.

11  John Frankenstein, 'China's Defense Industries: A New Course?', in James C. Mulvenon and Richard H. Yang (eds), *The People's Liberation Army in the Information Age* (Santa Monica, CA: RAND, 1999), pp. 191–92.

12  Department of Defence (Republic of South Africa), *White Paper on the South African Defence-Related Industries*, Chapter II, March 1998, available at: www.gov.za/whitepaper/1998/defence/defence.html

13  Steinberg, 'Israel', p. 172; Ralph Sanders, *Arms Industries: New Suppliers and Regional Security* (Washington DC: NDU Press, 1990), p. 53.

14  Elisabeth Sköns and Fredrik Wetterqvist, 'The Gripen and Sweden's Evolving Defense Industrial Policy', in Randall Forsberg (ed.), *The Arms Production Dilemma* (Cambridge, MA: MIT Press, 1994), pp. 225–26; 'Swedish Defense Industry Overview', *Advantage Sweden*, *Defense News* special supplement, May 1997, p. 16.

15  Ikegami-Andersson, *The Military-Industrial Complex*, quoting Ingemar Dörfer, p. 120.

16  James Elliot and Ezio Bonsignore,

'Asia's "New" Aerospace Industry: At the Turning Point?', *Military Technology*, February 1998, p. 31; Dean Cheng and Michael W. Chinworth, 'The Teeth of the Little Tigers: Offsets, Defense Production and Economic Development in South Korea and Taiwan', in Stephen Martin (ed.), *The Economics of Offsets: Defence Procurement and Countertrade* (London: Harwood, 1996), pp. 245–46.

[17] Steinberg, 'Israel', pp. 168–70; Sadeh, 'The Israeli Defense Industry', p. 3.

[18] Republic of Korea Ministry of National Defense, *Defense White Paper 1993–1994* (Seoul: Korea Institute for Defense Analyses, 1994), p. 192.

[19] 'Third World Arms Industries: Swords Not Ploughshares', *The Economist*, 23 March 1991.

[20] OTA, *Global Arms Trade*, p. 143.

[21] Ronnie Kasrils, 'The Future of South Africa's Defense Industry: The Government's Perspective', in William Gutteridge (ed.), *South Africa's Defense and Security into the 21st Century* (Dartmouth: Dartmouth Press, 1996), p. 121; Steinberg, 'Israel', pp. 181–88.

[22] Green, *Arming Japan*, pp. 11–13.

[23] Franko-Jones, *The Brazilian Defense Industry*, pp. 57.

[24] Cheng and Chinworth, 'The Teeth of the Little Tigers'; Kongdan Oh, 'US–Korea Aerospace Collaboration and the Korean Fighter Project', in Pia Christina Wood and David S. Sorenson (eds), *International Military Aerospace Collaboration: Case Studies in Domestic and International Politics* (Aldershot: Ashgate, 1999), p. 39.

[25] Krause, *Arms and the State*, p. 171; Michael Brzoska and Thomas Ohlson, 'Arms Production in the Third World: An Overview', in Brzoska and Ohlson (eds), *Arms Production in the Third World 1971–1985*, pp. 15–27; James Everett Katz, 'Understanding Arms Production in Developing Countries', in James Everett Katz (ed.), *Arms Production in Developing Countries: An Analysis of Decision Making* (Lexington, MA: Lexington Books, 1984), pp. 8–9; Willett, 'East Asia's Changing Defence Industry', pp. 116–18.

[26] Franko-Jones, *The Brazilian Defense Industry*, p. 148; OTA, *Global Arms Trade*, p. 143; Sanders, *Arms Industries: New Suppliers and Regional Security*, p. 33.

[27] In a rare twist in the usual North–South flow of military technologies, the UK during the 1980s manufactured *Tucanos* under licence from Embraer.

[28] Landgren, *Embargo Disimplemented*, pp. 67–68.

[29] *Ibid.*, pp. 73–75.

[30] McWilliams, *Armscor*, pp. 72–77.

[31] *Ibid.*, p. 179.

[32] Taken from the Kentron website (www.kentron.co.za), 17 March 2002.

[33] Oh, 'US–Korea Aerospace Collaboration', pp. 42–47; 'FX Fighter Program To Set Stage for Air Force Modernization Plan', *Aviation Week & Space Technology*, 12 June 1989, pp. 191–99.

[34] 'Korea's Golden Eagle Prepares To Leave the Nest', *International Defense Review*, September 2000.

[35] 'FX Fighter Program To Set Stage', p. 199; Cheng and Chinworth, 'The Teeth of the Little Tigers', p. 253.

[36] Brian Hsu, 'New Anti-Ship Missile Expected To Enter Production', *Taipei Times*, 12

September 2000, p. 3; Forecast International, 'Hsiung Feng I/II', *Missile Forecast*, June 1999; 'Taiwan Puts $600m into Missile Programs', *Jane's Defence Weekly*, 10 March 1999.

37 Brian Hsu, 'Report Says Military Developing New Missile', *Taipei Times*, 8 September 2000, p. 3; Robert Karniol, 'Taipei Develops Anti-Radiation Missile for Ching-Kuo IDF', *Jane's Defense Weekly*, 13 September 2000.

38 Klaus-Richard Böhme, 'The Principal Features of Swedish Defense Policy, 1925–1945', *Neutrality and Defense: The Swedish Experience*, special edition of *Revue Internationale D'Histoire Militaire*, no. 57, Stockholm, 1984, pp. 122–23, 127–28.

39 'Fourth-generation-plus' fighters fall between 1970s-era fourth-generation fighters (such as the F-16) and 1990s-era fifth-generation fighters (such as the F-22). They generally feature an unstable, fly-by-wire flight-control system, a canard-wing design, the extensive use of composite materials and some low-observability technologies. Other fourth-generation-plus fighters include the French *Rafale* and the Anglo-German-Italian-Spanish *Eurofighter Typhoon*, neither of which will enter service until the early 2000s.

40 Ikegami-Andersson, *The Military-Industrial Complex*, pp. 70–71; Kwang-il Baek and Chung-in Moon, 'Technological Dependence, Supplier Control and Strategies for Recipient Autonomy: The Case of South Korea', in Kwang-il Baek, Ronald. D. McLaurin and Chung-in Moon (eds), *The Dilemma of Third World Defense Industries* (Boulder, CO:

Westview Press, 1989), p. 158.

41 *Ibid.*, pp. 158–59; OTA, *Global Arms Trade*, p. 131.

42 Virginia C. Lopez and David H. Vadas, *After the Cold War: The US Aerospace Industry in the International Marketplace*, Part II (Washington DC: Aerospace Industries Association of America, 1994), pp. 31–32.

43 The Swedish Air Force, for example, is committed to purchasing 204 *Gripens* – a large number for a country of only eight million people and military expenditures of less than $5bn. In comparison, the UK, with a defence budget seven times bigger than Sweden's, is buying 232 *Eurofighters*.

44 OTA, *Global Arms Trade*, pp. 148–49.

45 Brzoska, 'South Africa: Evading the Embargo', p. 206.

46 Landgren, *Embargo Disimplemented*, pp. 75–77.

47 *Ibid.*, pp. 63–112; Forecast International, 'South Africa: Air-to-Air Missiles: V3A/B Kukri and V3C Darter', *Missile Forecast*, December 1998, p. 5.

48 Cheng and Chinworth, 'The Teeth of the Little Tigers', p. 258.

49 'Korea's Golden Eagle'.

50 Cheng and Chinworth, 'The Teeth of the Little Tigers', p. 255; OTA, *Global Arms Industry*, p. 136.

51 Cheng and Chinworth, 'The Teeth of the Little Tigers', p. 254.

52 Ingemar N. Dörfer, 'Technology and Military Doctrine in the Future of Swedish Defense', in Ciro Elliot Zoppo (ed.), *Nordic Security at the Turn of the Twenty-first Century* (New York: Greenwood, 1992), p. 138.

53 Nolan, *Military Industry in Taiwan and South Korea*, pp. 51–53; Cheng and Chinworth, 'The

Teeth of the Little Tigers', p. 258, 271–272; Masako Ikegami-Andersson, 'Japan', in Ravinder Pal Singh (ed.), *Arms Procurement Decision Making, Volume I*, pp. 155–57; Paul H. B. Godwin and Bernard D. Cole, 'Advanced Military Technology and the PLA: Priorities and Capabilities for the 21st Century', in Larry M. Wortzel (ed.), *The Chinese Armed Forces in the 21st Century* (Carlisle Barracks, PA: Strategic Studies Institute, 1999), pp. 159–215.

54 Eric Arnett, 'Military Research and Development', *SIPRI Yearbook 1996* (Oxford University Press for SIPRI, 1996), pp. 212, 215.

55 *SIPRI Yearbook 2001* (Oxford: Oxford University Press for SIPRI, 2001), p. 232.

56 Swedish Ministry of Defence press release, *The New Defence*, 25 November 1999, pp. 4–5; author's interviews in Sweden, May 2000.

57 Peter Batchelor, 'Disarmament and Defense Industrial Adjustment: The Case of South Africa's Defense Industry', paper presented to the Council on Foreign Relations, New York, January 1998, pp. 13–14; *White Paper on the South African Defence-Related Industries*, Chapter II.

58 Between 1991 and 1995, real Japanese defence procurement spending dropped by 6.2%, and it fell a further 1.8% between 1996 and 2000. Military R&D spending fell 8% during the period 1995–98. Masako Ikegami-Anderson, 'Globalization of Defense Industries: Sweden and Japan', paper presented to the Atlantic Council conference on 'Defense Industry Globalization', Washington DC, 16 November 2001, pp. 1, 15.

59 Willett, 'East Asia's Changing Defence Industry', p. 118.

60 Krause, *Arms and the State*, pp. 173–74.

61 Three US analysts assert that there even exists a growing technology gap *within* the first-tier of leading arms-producing countries. According to them, the major European allies (France, Germany, Italy and the UK) are falling far behind the US in harnessing the key information-based technologies of the new revolution in military affairs (RMA). Not only are the Europeans spending too little on RMA-related military R&D, they also lack both a 'vibrant information technology market' and defence industries that are 'agile enough to buy the best from that market'. As a result, 'European forces cannot acquire information-age capabilities from industries that are not able consistently to provide them at affordable prices'. David C. Gompert, Richard L. Kugler and Martin C. Libicki, *Mind the Gap: Promoting a Transatlantic Revolution in Military Affairs* (Washington DC: National Defense University Press, 1999), pp. 11–12.

62 Krause, *Arms and the State*, p. 168; Willett, 'East Asia's Changing Defence Industry', pp. 118–21; Stephanie G. Neuman, 'International Stratification and Third World Military Industries', *International Organization*, Winter 1984, p. 178.

63 Nolan, *Military Industry in Taiwan and South Korea*, pp. 63–66; Cheng and Chinworth, 'The

Teeth of the Little Tigers', p. 276.

[64] Baek and Moon, 'Technological Dependence, Supplier Control and Strategies for Recipient Autonomy', p. 182.

[65] Krause, *Arms and the State*, pp. 163–68.

[66] Ikegami-Andersson, 'Japan', pp. 155–57.

[67] Mark Lorell, *Troubled Partnership: A History of US–Japan Collaboration on the FS-X Fighter* (Santa Monica, CA: RAND, 1995), p. 283.

[68] Dong Joon Hwang, 'Economic Interdependence and its Impact on National Security: Defense Industry Cooperation and Technology Transfer', paper presented to the National Defense University Pacific Symposium, Washington DC, 27–28 February 1992, pp. 12–14.

[69] Franko-Jones, *The Brazilian Defense Industry*, p. 196; Phil Finnegan, 'S. Korea's New Trainer Jet Faces Tough Market', *Defense News*, 13 March 2000.

[70] Green, *Arming Japan*, pp. 17–20; Elliot and Bonsignore, 'Asia's "New" Aerospace Industry', pp. 24, 31–32.

[71] Yongwook Jun, 'The Win–Win Strategy of the Industrial Alliance Between the Korean and US Aeronautics Industry', paper presented to the conference 'An Industrial Alliance Between the United States and Korea', La Jolla, CA, 22–24 June 1994, p. 19.

[72] Author's interviews in South Korea, May 2000 and December 1994; Bruce Dorminey, 'Industry Watches as Korea Consolidates', *Aviation Week & Space Technology*, 2 November 1998; South Korean Ministry of National Defense, *Defense White Paper 1999: Republic of Korea*

(Seoul: Korea Institute for Defense Analyses, 1999), p. 148; Bruce Dorminey, 'Government Spurns Korean Business Plan', *Aviation Week & Space Technology*, 14 December 1998, pp. 20–31.

[73] Brent Hannon, 'Changing the Guard: Taiwan's Aerospace Industry Is Facing Up to the Realities of New Privatization', *Flight International*, 5 March 1997, pp. 49–50.

[74] Franko-Jones, *The Brazilian Defense Industry*, p. 196; Evans, 'Reappraising Third-World Arms Production', p. 107.

[75] Yongwook Jun, 'The Win–Win Strategy', pp. 21–22.

[76] Frankenstein and Gill, 'Current and Future Challenges Facing Chinese Defense Industries', p. 403; Frankenstein, 'China's Defense Industries', pp. 197–99.

[77] US Arms Control and Disarmament Agency (ACDA), *World Military Expenditures and Arms Transfers 1996* (Washington DC: USGPO, 1996), Table II, p. 113.

[78] Jurgen Brauer, 'Arms Production in Developing Nations: The Relation to Industrial Structure, Industrial Diversification, and Human Capital Formation', *Defense Economics*, vol. 2, 1991, p. 166.

[79] *Ibid.*

[80] Baek and Moon, 'Technological Dependence, Supplier Control and Strategies for Recipient Autonomy', p. 158.

[81] Ian Anthony, 'The "Third Tier" Countries: Production of Major Weapons', in Herbert Wulf (ed.), *Arms Industry Limited* (Oxford: Oxford University Press, 1993), p. 365; Baek and Moon, 'Technological Dependence', p. 157; South Korean Ministry of

National Defense, *Defense White Paper 1998: Republic of Korea* (Seoul: Korea Institute for Defense Analyses, 1998), p. 160.

[82] Neuman, 'International Stratification and Third World Military Industries', pp. 180–81.

[83] Krause, *Arms and the State*, pp. 172–74; Neuman, 'International Stratification and Third World Military Industries', pp. 180–81; Herbert Wulf, 'Developing Countries', in Nicole Ball and Milton Leitenberg (eds), *The Structure of the Defence Industry* (London: St Martin's Press, 1983), p. 330.

[84] Krause, *Arms and the State*, p. 172.

[85] Katz, 'Understanding Arms Production in Developing Countries', p. 8.

[86] Willett, 'East Asia's Changing Defence Industry', p. 117.

[87] *Ibid*.

[88] Elliot and Bonsignore, 'Asia's "New" Aerospace Industry', p. 31.

[89] It has been long established that, even among the first-tier arms-producing countries, most major weapon systems are exponentially more expensive than the system they replace; of course, successor generations of weaponry tend to be exponentially more capable as well. See Edward A. Kolodziej, *Making and Marketing Arms: The French Experience and Its Implications for the International System* (Princeton, NJ: Princeton University Press, 1987), pp. 140–43. At the same time, first-tier states are better situated to deal with these rising opportunity costs, due to their higher levels of defence spending and innate strengths in defence R&D, as well as their growing predilection for joint development and production of advanced weapon systems.

[90] Saadet Deger, *Military Expenditure in Third World Countries: The Economic Effects* (London: Routledge & Kegan Paul, 1986), p. 177.

[91] Neuman, 'International Stratification and Third World Military Industries', p. 189; Brzoska and Ohlson, 'Conclusions', in Brzoska and Ohlson (eds), *Arms Production in the Third World 1971–1985*, p. 283.

[92] *Forsvarsstatisik 1989* (Stockholm: Ministry of Defence, 1989); US ACDA, *World Military Expenditures and Arms Transfers 1998* (Washington DC: USGPO, 1999), Table II.

[93] Franko-Jones, *The Brazilian Defense Industry*, p. 195.

[94] *Ibid.*, pp. 195–98.

**Chapter 2**

[1] 'Swedish Defense Industry Overview', p. 17.

[2] *White Paper on the South African Defence-Related Industries*, Chapter IV.

[3] *1993–94 National Defense Report: Republic of China* (Taipei: Ministry of National Defence, 1994), p. 152.

[4] *Defense White Paper 1998: Republic of Korea*, pp. 160, 248.

[5] Richard A. Bitzinger, 'Globalization in the Post-Cold War Defense Industry: Challenges and Opportunities', in Ann R. Markusen and Sean S. Costigan (eds), *Arming the Future: A Defense Industry for the 21st Century* (New York: Council on Foreign Relations, 1999), pp. 305–33; Keith Hayward, 'The Globalization of Defense Industries', *Survival*,

Summer 2001, pp. 115–32.

6  Luis Bittencourt, 'Brazil Must Build Defense-Industry Muscle', *Jane's Defence Weekly*, 21 June 2000, p. 26.

7  Franko-Jones, *The Brazilian Defense Industry*, p. 189; OTA, *Global Arms Trade*, p. 149.

8  Forecast International, 'MAF/MSS 1.2', *Missile Forecast*, September 1999, pp. 1, 3–4; 'Additional Worldwide Missile Programs', *ibid.*, 1 January 1 2000, p. 4.

9  'Avibras Sells Astros Rockets, Vehicles to Malaysia', *Epoca* (Rio de Janeiro), 14 May 2001, in *FBIS*, 18 May 2001; Luis Bittencourt, 'Brazil Must Build Defense-Industry Muscle', *Jane's Defence Weekly*, 21 June 2000, p. 26.

10  Wyn Q. Brown, 'Brazil's Accession to the MTCR' *Nonproliferation Review* (internet version), Spring/Summer 1996.

11  Joanna Kidd, 'Brazilian Naval Ambitions', *IISS Strategic Pointers*, 26 July 2000.

12  Embraer website, 17 March 2002, www.embraer.com.

13  'Brazil Is In the Pilot's Seat as the Small Jet Market Takes Off', *The Times*, 7 October 1999.

14  Embraer website, 17 March 2002, www.embraer.com.

15  'Brazil Is In the Pilot's Seat'.

16  Embraer website, 17 March 2002, www.embraer.com.

17  'Brazil Awards $420 Million Contract to Embraer for Super Tucano Aircraft', *Defense Daily International* (internet version), 10 August 2001.

18  Embraer website, 22 March 2000, www.embraer.com.

19  'Brazilian Maker of Jet Aircraft May Sell Stake to Foreigners', *Wall Street Journal*, 14 September 1999; 'Embraer "Sell-Out" Claims Dismissed by French', *Jane's Defence Weekly*,

5 January 2000, p. 21.

20  Embraer website, 14 November 2001, www.embraer.com.

21  *White Paper on the South African Defence-Related Industries*, Chapter II.

22  Author's interviews in South Africa, May 2000.

23  Batchelor, 'Disarmament and Defense Industrial Adjustment', pp. 6, 15, 17; *White Paper on the South African Defence-Related Industries*, Chapter II; 'South Africa: Industry Waits On the Edge', *Jane's Defence Weekly*, 11 November 1998.

24  *White Paper on the South African Defence-Related Industries*, Chapter II.

25  Batchelor, 'Disarmament and Defense Industrial Adjustment', pp. 19–33; *White Paper on the South African Defence-Related Industries*, Chapter II.

26  Author's interviews in South Africa, May 2000.

27  Peter Batchelor and Susan Willett, *Disarmament and Defence Industrial Adjustment in South Africa* (Oxford: Oxford University Press, 1998), pp. 159–63; author's interviews in South Africa, May 2000.

28  Helmoed-Rämer Heitman, 'South African Industry Finding its Footing Again', *Jane's Defence Weekly*, 18 August 2000.

29  'Denel Lifts Exports 26.4% to R1.3 Billion', *Johannesburg Star*, 17 August 2000; author's interviews in South Africa, May 2000.

30  Denel website, 17 March 2002, www.denel.co.za.

31  Batchelor, 'Disarmament and Defense Industrial Adjustment', p. 20.

32  'Pretoria Insists Denel Will Be Privatized', *Defense News*, 21 August 2000, p. 2.

33  Greg Mills and Martin

Edmonds, 'South Africa's Defense Industry: A Template for Middle Powers?', paper presented to paper delivered to the IISS/NIC conference on 'Transformation in Global Defense Markets and Industries', London, 4–5 November 2000, p. 9.

34 Author's interviews in South Africa, May 2000.

35 Keith Campbell, 'South Africa Confirms SANDF Re-equipment Program', *Military Technology*, November 1999, pp. 34, 36–37; 'South Africa Signs Orders For $5 Billion', *Jane's Defence Weekly*, 8 December 1999; 'South African Companies Share in Defense Deals', *ibid.*, 29 September 1999.

36 Campbell, 'South Africa Confirms SANDF Re-equipment Program'; author's interviews in South Africa, May 2000.

37 'SA Set To Benefit from Czech Arms Deal', 10 December 2001, *Sapa* (internet version); 'Sweden Procuring 20 A109 Power Helos', *Helicopter News*, 12 July 2001, p. 1.

38 'South Africa: Industry Waits On the Edge'; 'S. African Arms Maker Wants BAE or EADS As Partners', *Reuters*, 15 March 2000; 'DASA Takes 33 pct Stake in South Africa's Reutech Radar Systems', *AFX*, 12 August 1999; 'Celsius and Grintek Establish EW Joint Venture', *Journal of Electronic Defense*, April 1999; Batchelor, 'Disarmament and Defense Industrial Adjustment', p. 32.

39 'Pretoria Insists Denel Will Be Privatized.'

40 Author's interviews in South Africa, May 2000.

41 *Defence White Paper 1999: Republic of Korea*, p. 145.

42 'MND FY99 Support for ROK Defense Industry', *Kukpang-Kwa Kisul* (Seoul), 1 April 1999, pp. 10–11, *FBIS*, 11 May 1999.

43 'The Shaking F-X Program', *Chungang Ilbo* (internet version), 17 April 2001, *FBIS*, 19 April 2001); Shim-jae Hoon, 'South Korean Projects May Face Further Delays', *Jane's Defence Weekly*, 18 April 2001; Hwang Jang-jin, 'Portable Missile Developed', *Korea Herald*, 29 November 2001.

44 *Defense White Paper 2000: Republic of Korea* (internet version), Chapter 2, 'Defense Investment Projects for State-of-the-Art Weapons Systems', and Appendix.

45 Author's interviews in South Korea, March 2000; *Defense White Paper 1998: Republic of Korea*, pp. 160–62; *Defense White Paper 1999: Republic of Korea*, pp. 148–49.

46 Paul Lewis, 'South Korean Trio Start Single-Entity Talks', *Flight International*, 21 October 1998, p. 28; 'KAI To Receive 530 Billion Won in Financial Support', *Yonhap*, 19 December 2000, *FBIS*, 19 December 2000; Philip Finnegan, 'Diverging Industrial Policies: South Korea and Taiwan Adjust to Aerospace Defense Globalization', paper presented to the Atlantic Council conference on 'The Globalization of the Defense Industry', Washington DC, 16 November 2001, p. 5.

47 Robert Wall and Geoffrey Thomas, 'South Korea Sets Ambitious Plans', *Aviation Week & Space Technology*, 21 February 2000, p. 91; Cho 'Korea Unveils New-Look Aerospace Industry', pp. 18–21.

48 'Government's Decision To Offer Priority to KAI Creates Backlash', *Korea Herald*,

9 February 2000.

49 Korea Aerospace Industries website, 17 March 2002, www.koreaaero.com; Myeong-Chin Cho, 'Korea Unveils New-Look Aerospace Industry', *Interavia*, February 2000, pp. 20–21; 'ROK To Step Up Development of Domestic Aerospace Industry', *Yonhap*, 22 April 1999.

50 Philip Finnegan, 'S. Korea's New Trainer Jet Faces Tough Market', *Defense News*, 13 March 2000.

51 Finnegan, 'Diverging Industrial Policies', p. 3; Cheng and Chinworth, 'The Teeth of the Little Tigers', p. 269.

52 *Yonhap*, 'KAI to Receive 530 Billion Won in Financial Support;' Finnegan, 'Diverging Industrial Policies', p. 9.

53 Finnegan, 'Diverging Industrial Policies', p. 6; 'Mergers & Acquisitions, Korea', *Jane's Defence Industry*, December 1999.

54 Finnegan, 'Diverging Industrial Policies', p. 7; 'KAI To Receive 530 Billion Won.'

55 Derived from the *Korean Defense Products Guide* (Seoul: Korea Defense Industry Association, 1999).

56 Author's interviews in South Korea, March 2000.

57 Choe Seung-chul, 'Samsung Aerospace Shifting Focus to Chip, Optical-Digital Equipment', *Korea Herald*, 22 December 1999.

58 'Air Force Protests Decision To Produce Older Jet Fighters', *Korea Times*, 12 May 1999; Geoffrey Thomas, 'Koreans Face Dilemma on Fighter Production', *Aviation Week & Space Technology*, 12 April 1999, p. 71; 'S. Korean Air Force Considers Stopgap Fighter', *Flight International*, 26 August 1999, p. 16; 'The Shaking F-X Program'.

59 'ROK Suspends Mid-Sized Aircraft Project', *Yonhap*, 27 April 1999. Both international programmes eventually collapsed in any event, though for other reasons.

60 Dorminey, 'Industry Watches as Korea Consolidates.'

61 'KAI to Receive 530 Billion Won in Financial Support'; 'Boeing Continues Korea Aerospace Investment Push Without BAE', *Bloomberg Business News Agency*, 9 May 2001.

62 Robert Karniol, 'S. Korea's Exports Rise', *Jane's Defence Weekly*, 23 February 2000.

63 M.G. Mahmud, 'The South Korean Defense Industry Consolidates for the Future', *Asian Defence Journal*, October 2001, pp. 34–36.

64 Nolan, 'South Korea', pp. 225–27.

65 'KAI Exports Trainer Aircraft for the First Time', *Yonhap*, 26 February 2001; Yi Chong-hun, 'Exporting Is the Only Way To Survive', *Sisa Journal*, 29 August 1996, p. 34, *FBIS*, 29 August 1996.

66 *Defense White Paper 1998: Republic of Korea*, p. 163.

67 'ROK Outperforms Japan in Shipbuilding in 1999', *Korea Herald*, 31 January 2000; author's interviews in South Korea, March 2000.

68 Finnegan, 'Diverging Industrial Policies', p. 8.

69 Author's interviews in Seoul, March 2000.

70 Author's interviews in Seoul, March 2000.

71 Author's interviews in Seoul, March 2000.

72 'Interview with Owe Wiktoren, Supreme Commander of the Swedish Armed Forces', *Advantage Sweden*, p. 17.

73 'Interview with Birgitta Böhlin,

Director-General of FMV',
*Military Technology*, February
2000, p. 18.

[74] Saab AB website: http://
www.saab.se/node966.asp
(accessed 2.4.03)

[75] Gunnar Lindstedt and Sune
Olofson, 'Top Military
Commander Saving Money on
New Weapons', *Svenska Dagbladet*
(internet version), 17 February
1998; additional information
provided by the Swedish Defence
Industry Association
(*Försvarsindustriförening*), the
SIPRI arms production database,
the French General Delegation
for Armaments (DGA) and
annual reports for Celsius
Industries and Saab.

[76] Author's interviews in Sweden,
May 2000.

[77] *Saab: Northern Europe's Leading
High Technology Company*, p. 7.

[78] *Ibid*.

[79] *Saab Annual Report, 1998*
(Linköping: Saab Technologies,
1999), pp. 44–45.

[80] *Saab: Northern Europe's Leading
High Technology Company*, p. 14;
Tim Burt, 'Celsius Looks to
Catch the Defence
Consolidation Wave', *Financial
Times*, 27 August 1998, p. 18.

[81] *Saab: Northern Europe's Leading
High Technology Company*,
pp. 2–5, 9.

[82] Author's interviews in Sweden,
May 2000.

[83] In constant 1997 dollars. US
ACDA, *World Military
Expenditures and Arms Transfers*
for 1998 and various years;
Sköns and Wetterqvist, 'The
Gripen', p. 230.

[84] Data provided by the Swedish
Defence Industry Association;
*Advantage Sweden*, p. 17.

[85] Saab has traditionally relied
upon the Swedish Air Force for
its combat-aircraft market, and
it managed to sell only a
handful of J-29 *Tunnans*, Saab-
105s, and J-35 *Drakens* abroad –
and then to just three countries
(Austria, Denmark and Finland)
– while not a single *Viggen* was
exported. According to one
analyst, even when there was a
prospect in the mid-1970s of
exporting hundreds of *Viggens*
to four Western European air
forces (Belgium, Denmark,
Netherlands and Norway), the
Swedish industry and
government never really had its
heart in the effort, and the sale
eventually went to the F-16; see
Ingemar Dörfer, *Arms Deal: The
Selling of the F-16* (New York:
Praeger, 1983), pp. 178–92.

[86] *Saab Annual Report, 1998*, p. 33;
Joris Janssen Lok, 'Upgrades
Will Lift Gripen into Next
Decade', *International Defense
Review*, July 2000, pp. 26–31;
author's interviews in Sweden,
May 2000.

[87] *The New Defence*, p. 9.

[88] Björn Hagelin, 'Saab, British
Aerospace, and the JAS 39
Gripen Aircraft Joint Venture',
*European Security*, Winter 1998,
pp. 91–117.

[89] *The New Defence*, p. 9.

[90] Author's interviews in Sweden,
May 2000; author's interview
with a Swedish defence official
in Washington DC, April 2000.

[91] 'Interview with Birgitta Böhlin',
p. 18.

[92] 'Li Teng-Hui Calls for Home
Weapons Development', *AFP*
(Hong Kong), 1 July 1999.

[93] 'Former CSIST Chief Calls for
Domestic Military', *CNA*
(internet version), in English,
8 August 2000.

[94] Hannon, 'Changing the Guard',
p. 49; 'Taiwan Institute Cutting

Back Sharply Due to Foreign Supply', *The Estimate*, 10 June 1994, p. 4.

95 Andrzej Jeziorski, 'AIDC Still Aims for Privatization', *Flight International*, 25 August 1999, p. 23.

96 'Taiwan: Industry Plays Vital Part in Modernization', *Jane's Defence Weekly*, 8 July 1998; Kelly Her, 'Military Producer of IDFs Changing into Private Firm', *Free China Journal*, 20 October 1995, p. 3.

97 Author's interviews in Taiwan, September 2000.

98 *TAC/Taiwan Aerospace Corporation*, undated brochure; 'Taiwan Aerospace May Lease', *Asian Wall Street Journal*, 15 May 1996.

99 'Taichung To Become Aerospace Industrial Area', *CNA* (internet edition), 6 November 1999.

100 AIDC website, 17 March 2002, www.aidc.com.tw; 'AIDC, Sikorsky To Coproduce D-92 Choppers', *CNA* (internet edition), 6 February 1998; 'Taiwan, Czech Republic Form Plane-Making Venture', *Reuters*, 15 March 1997.

101 'Taiwanese Firms Poise To Make Push into Offset Component Manufacturing', *Asian Aviation*, July 1992, pp. 11–12; 'AIDC Stepping Up Production of Boeing Parts', *China News*, 2 August 1999; AIDC website, 17 March 2002, www.aidc.com.tw.

102 Robert Karniol, 'Taiwan Postpones Aerospace Privatization', *Jane's Defence Weekly*, 4 October 2000.

103 Author's interviews in Taiwan, September 2000.

104 'Government Enterprises Facing Pressure To Liberalize', *CNA* (internet edition), in English, 14 May 1999.

105 *1998 National Defense Report: Republic of China*, pp. 113, 139;

Wu Nan-Shan, 'President Lee Stresses Building Independent Defense Industry as Established Policy, and Calls for Developing Defense Industry by Utilizing Civilian Resources', *Chung Kuo Shih Pao* (Taipei), 28 November 1992, p. 6, in *FBIS-CHI-92-235*, 7 December 1992, p. 57; author's interviews in Taiwan, August 1995.

106 Andrzej Jeziorski, 'Aero Vodochody Flies Initial Combat Version of L-159', *Flight International*, 26 August 1999, p. 16; Karniol, 'Taiwan Postpones Aerospace Privatization.'

107 'AIDC Begins Design of IDF Trainer', *ibid.*, 24 November 1999, p. 28.

108 'AIDC Seeks Strategic Investors for Privatization', *CNA* (internet edition), 4 August 1998; Jeziorski, 'AIDC Still Aims for Privatization'; Karniol, 'Taiwan Postpones Aerospace Privatization.'

109 Chris Pocock, 'Taiwan Government Uncertain on Plans for Top Aerospace Firm', *Aviation International News*, 22 February 2000, p. 34; Jeziorski, 'AIDC Still Aims for Privatization'; Andrzej Jeziorski, 'Weathering the Storm', *Flight International*, 11 August 1999.

110 Author's interviews in Taiwan, September 2000.

111 'Taiwan: Industry Plays Vital Part in Modernization', *Jane's Defence Weekly*, 8 July 1998.

112 *Ibid.*; Hannon, 'Changing the Guard'.

113 George O'Young, 'China Shipbuilding Facing Difficult Times', *Taiwan News*, 18 September 2000, p. 16; 'China Shipbuilding Corporation Out of Red', *CNA*, 23 September 2002.

114 Department of State, Bureau of Verification and Compliance,

*World Military Expenditures and Arms Transfers 1998* (Washington DC: USGPO, 2000), p. 129.

[115]Philip Finnegan, 'Taiwan in Lonely Quest for Foreign Sales, Investors', *Defense News*, 3 April 2000.

[116]Author's interviews in Taiwan, September 2000.

[117]'AIDC, AIR Development of 70-Seat Aircraft Viewed', *CNA* (internet edition), 10 November 1996; 'Taiwan Company Won't Take Stake in Airbus Jet', *Seattle Times*, 3 July 2001, p. C2.

[118]Jeziorski, 'Weathering the Storm'.

[119]'In Brief', *AA2000 Today*, 24 February 2000, p. 15.

[120]Author's interviews in Taiwan, September 2000; Wendell Minnick, 'Taiwan Finalizes Design for Fast Attack Craft', *ibid.*, 12 April 2000.

[121]Wendell Minnick, 'Taiwan's Strike Aircraft Plan', *Jane's Defence Weekly*, 9 August 2000.

[122]Wendell Minnick, 'Taiwan To Produce 100 Thunder 2000s', *ibid.*, 9 August 2000; 'Cross-Strait Sea Supremacy Forces Compared', *Chien-Tuan K'e-chi* (Taipei), 1 January 1999, in *FBIS*, 15 February 1999; 'How Can We Counter the "Hsiung Feng 2"?', *Jianchuan Zhishi* (Beijing), 4 September 1999, in *FBIS*, 15 October 1999; Bryan Bender and Robert Karniol, 'Taiwan Puts $600m into Missile Programs', *Jane's Defence Weekly*, 10 March 1999; author's interviews in Taiwan, September 2000.

**Chapter 3**

1  Vivek Raghuvanshi, 'India's Light Fighter Effort Faces More Delays', *Defense News*, 8 May 2000, p. 20; Vivek Raghuvanshi, 'India Panel Raps Indigenous Effort', *ibid.*, 8 May 2000, p. 28; Chris Smith, *India's Ad Hoc Arsenal: Direction or Drift in Defence Policy?* (Oxford: Oxford University Press, 1994), pp. 144–78.

2  OTA, *After the Cold War: Living With Lower Defense Spending* (Washington DC: USGPO, 1992), pp. 204–17.

3  Willett, 'Globalization and the East Asian Defense Market', pp. 17–18.

4  Richard A. Bitzinger and Steven M. Kosiak, *Windows of Opportunity: The Potential Military Application of Japanese Advanced Commercial Technology Transfers to East Asia* (Washington DC: Defense Budget Project, September 1995), pp. 33–43; Green, *Arming Japan*, pp. 125–52.

5  Cohen, 'New Flight Plan'; Cho, 'Korea Unveils New-Look Aerospace Industry'; author's interviews in Sweden, May 2000.

6  Bitzinger, 'Globalization in the Post-Cold War Defense Industry', pp. 310–20.

7  Hayward, 'The Globalization of Defense Industries', pp. 116–23.

8  Author's interviews in South Africa, May 2000.

9  Green, *Arming Japan*, pp. 156–58; one exception is Japan's decision to develop two new maritime patrol and transport aircraft.

10  See, for example, Immanuel Wallerstein, 'The Future of the World-Economy', in Terence K. Hopkins and Immanuel Wallerstein (eds), *Processes of the World-System* (Beverly Hills, CA: Sage, 1980), pp. 167–80.

11  Author's interviews in South Africa and Sweden, May 2000.

12  'In Brief', *AA2000 Today*, 24 February 2000, p. 15.

13  See 'Going Places or Running in Place? China's Efforts to

Leverage Advanced Technologies for Military Use', in Susan Puska (ed.), *The PLA After Next* (Carlisle Barracks, PA: SSI Press, 2000).

14 Jonathan Pollack and James Mulvenon, *Assembled in China: Sino-US Collaboration and the Chinese Civilian Aviation Industry*, draft manuscript (Santa Monica, CA: RAND, 1998), p. 16; *China Daily*, 31 January 1999.

15 Richard A. Bitzinger, 'Military Spending and Foreign Military Acquisitions by the PRC and Taiwan', in James R. Lilley and Chuck Downs (eds), *Crisis in the Taiwan Strait* (Washington DC: National Defense University Press, 1997), p. 92.

16 Damon Bristow, 'Globalization Versus Self-Reliance in India's Defense Industry – Can the Conflict Be Resolved', paper presented to the Atlantic Council conference on 'The Globalization of Defense Industries', Washington DC, 16 November 2001.

17 Raymond Vernon and Ethan B. Kapstein, 'National Needs, Global Resources', *Daedalus*, Autumn 1991, p. 19.

## Conclusion

1 Bitzinger, 'Globalization in the Post-Cold War Defense Industry', pp. 325–27; Keith Hayward, 'Globalization, the Revolution in Military Affairs, and the Future of the World Defense Industrial System', paper presented to the IISS/ NIC conference on 'Transformation in Global Defense Markets and Industries', London, 4–5 November 2000, pp. 6–8.

2 Finnegan, 'S. Korea's New Trainer Jet Faces Tough Market'.

3 Krause, *Arms and the State*, p. 19.

4 *Ibid.*, pp. 18–26; Robert Gilpin, *War and Change in World Politics* (Cambridge: Cambridge University Press, 1981), pp. 175–85.

5 Ann Markusen, 'The Rise of World Weapons', *Foreign Affairs*, Spring 1999, p. 41.

6 Gordon Adams, 'Fortress America in a Changing Transatlantic Defence Market', in Burkard Schmitt (ed.), *Between Cooperation and Competition: The Transatlantic Defence Market*, Chailott Paper 44 (Paris: Western European Union, Institute for Security Studies, January 2001), pp. 43–47.

7 Paul Dibb, 'The Future Military Capabilities of Asia's Great Powers', *Jane's Intelligence Review*, May 1995, p. 229.

8 Hayward, 'Globalization', p. 20.

9 *Ibid.*; see also Hayward, 'The Globalization of Defence Industries', p. 127.